CULTURES OF THE WORLD
Tahiti

Cavendish
Square
New York

Published in 2018 by Cavendish Square Publishing, LLC
243 5th Avenue, Suite 136, New York, NY 10016

Website: cavendishsq.com

This publication represents the opinions and views of the author based on his or her personal experience, knowledge, and research. The information in this book serves as a general guide only. The author and publisher have used their best efforts in preparing this book and disclaim liability rising directly or indirectly from the use and application of this book.

Cataloging-in-Publication Data

Names: NgCheong-Lum, Roseline. | Nevins, Debbie.
Title: Tahiti / Roseline NgCheong-Lum and Debbie Nevins.
Description: New York : Cavendish Square, 2018. | Series: Cultures of the world (third edition) | Includes index.
Identifiers: ISBN 9781502627414 (library bound) | ISBN 9781502627353 (ebook)
Subjects: LCSH: Tahiti (French Polynesia : Island)--Juvenile literature.
Classification: LCC DU870.N49 2018 | DDC 996.2'11--dc23

Writers, Roseline NgCheong-Lum; Debbie Nevins, third edition
Editorial Director, third edition: David McNamara
Editor, third edition: Debbie Nevins
Art Director, third edition: Amy Greenan
Designer, third edition: Jessica Nevins

Picture Researcher, third edition: Jessica Nevins

PICTURE CREDITS

Cover: Jose Gil/Alamy
The photographs in this book are used with the permission of: p. 1 Kyle Rothenborg/Perspectives/Getty Images; p. 3 Denis Burdin/Shutterstock.com; p. 5 Rothenborg Kyle/Perspectives/Getty Images; p. 6 Tomas del Amo/Perspectives/Getty Images; p. 7 Paul Gauguin/Wikimedia Commons/File:Paul Gauguin 056.jpg/CC-PD-Mark; p. 9 Yvette Cardozo/Photolibrary/Getty Images; p. 10 dikobraziy/Shutterstock.com; p. 12 Rainer Lesniewski/Shutterstock.com; p. 13 KKulikov/Shutterstock.com; p. 14 Matt Houser/Shutterstock.com; p. 15 NASA/Wikimedia Commons/File:Makatea2.JPG; p. 16 KKulikov/Shutterstock.com; p. 17 Nenad Basic/Shutterstock.com; p. 19 GREGORY BOISSY/AFP/Getty Images; p. 20 Ophe/Shutterstock.com; p. 21 Steve Oehlenschlager/Shutterstock.com; p. 22 Earl & Nazima Kowall/Corbis Documentary/Getty Images; p. 25 Cristina Mittermeier/National Geographic/Getty Images; p. 26 Jodocus Hondius/Wikimedia Commons/File:AMH-6605-KB Map of the world in two globes.jpg/PD-Art; p. 28 Time Life Pictures/Mansell/The LIFE Picture Collection/Getty Images; p. 29 William Parry/Wikimedia Commons/File:Omai (Mai), Sir Joseph Banks and Daniel Charles Solander; p. 30 Robert Dodd/Wikimedia Commons/File:HMS Bounty.jpg; p. 31 EuroCarGT/Wikimedia Commons/File:Pomare II, engraving by R. Hicks.jpg; p. 32 Max Radiguet/Wikimedia Commons/File:M. Radiguet, Proclamation du protectorat, Tahiti.jpg/CC-PD-Mark; p. 34 Keystone-France/Gamma-Keystone via Getty Images; p. 38 GREGORY BOISSY/AFP/Getty Images; p. 40 narvikk/E+/Getty Images; p. 41 Nightstallion/Wikimedia Commons/File:Flag of French Polynesia.svg; p. 42 GREGORY BOISSY/AFP/Getty Images; p. 43 GREGORY BOISSY/AFP/Getty Images); p. 44 Sergio Calleja/Wikimedia Commons/File:Pouvanaa a Oopa (Papeete - Tahiti).jpg/CC BY-SA 2.0; p. 45 Greg VaughnPerspectives/Getty Images; p. 46 sarayuth3390/Shutterstock.com; p. 47 Dan Kelleher/Shutterstock.com; p. 49 Andia/UIG via Getty Images; p. 50 Jason Loucas/Photolibrary/Getty Images; p. 51 Andia/UIG via Getty Images; p. 52 sarayuth3390/Shutterstock.com; p. 54 Eric Kulin/Perspectives/Getty Images; p. 55 Evil Monkey/Wikimedia Commons/File:Le Truck Papeete French Polynesia.JPG/CC-BY-2.5; p. 56 BlueOrange Studio/Shutterstock.com; p. 58 Atlantide Phototravel/Corbis Documentary/Getty Images; p. 61 MikhailSh/Shutterstock.com; p. 63 Joshua McCullough/Photolibrary/Getty Images; p. 64 Ian Trower/Alamy Stock Photo; p. 66 ChameleonsEye/Shutterstock.com; p. 69 Michael Maslan/Corbis/VCG via Getty Images; p. 71 philippe giraud/Sygma via Getty Images; p. 73 Michael Maslan/Corbis/VCG via Getty Images; p. 74 Tanee Nomai/Shutterstock.com; p. 77 Andia/UIG via Getty Images; p. 79 GREGORY BOISSY/AFP/Getty Images; p. 84 Sylvain Grandadam/Photographer's Choice/Getty Images; p. 90 Paul Gauguin/Wikimedia Commons/File:Maruru by Paul Gauguin.jpg/PD-US; p. 92 Paul Kennedy Lonely Planet Images/Getty Images; p. 94 Merten Snijders/Lonely Planet Images/Getty Images; p. 96 Weller/ullstein bild via Getty Images; p. 98 Purestock/Model released/Getty Images; p. 100 GREGORY BOISSY/AFP/Getty Images; p. 101 Xavier MARCHANT/Shutterstock.com; p. 103 Uladzik Kryhin/Shutterstock.com; p. 105 Paul Gauguin/Wikimedia Commons/File:Paul Gauguin, Nafea Faa Ipoipo? 1892, oil on canvas, 101 x 77 cm.jpg/CC-PD-Mark; p. 107 Xavier MARCHANT/Shutterstock.com; p. 108 GREGORY BOISSY/AFP/Getty Images; p. 109 Dario Diament/Shutterstock.com 110 DeAgostini/Getty Images; p. 111 Shaun Botterill - FIFA/FIFA via Getty Images; p. 112 Holger Leue/Lonely Planet Images/Getty Images; p. 114 Blaine Harrington III/Corbis Documentary/Getty Images; p. 120 Kletr/Shutterstock.com; p. 122 Holger Leue/Lonely Planet Images/Getty Images; p. 123 Calinat/Shutterstock.com; p. 124 Education Images/UIG via Getty Images; p. 125 Don Mammoser/Shutterstock.com; p. 126 Calinat/Shutterstock.com; p. 128 DANIEL BARQUERO/Shutterstock.com; p. 129 Holger Leue/Lonely Planet Images/Getty Images; p. 130 Tyler Nevins; p. 131 vsl/Shutterstock.com.

PRECEDING PAGE
A beach scene on Bora Bora.

Printed in the United States of America

CONTENTS

TAHITI TODAY

FOR MANY PEOPLE, THE WORD TAHITI CONJURES IMAGES OF A TROPICAL paradise. On this perfect island, waves lap soothingly on the white sand while palm trees bend gently in the warm breeze. The sun is bright on the blue-green sea. Beautiful women with flowers in their hair dance on the beach, their hips swaying to sweet music. No one has a care in the world.

That's the fantasy, and it's not a new one. Ever since European explorers "discovered" this island in the South Pacific in the late 1700s, they have portrayed it as an otherworldly idyll. For those sea-hardened men, far from the eighteenth-century Western world they knew as "civilization," the Tahitians were primitive and exotic. The half-naked people—by Western standards of dress—seemed mysterious, sensuous, and erotic; their lifestyle freer and closer to nature.

The French explorer Louis Antoine de Bougainville visited Tahiti in 1771 and named it New Cythera, after the Greek island where the mythological Aphrodite was said to be born. Aphrodite, remember, is the goddess of love, beauty, pleasure, and procreation. After months at sea with other filthy, sweating men inside a relentlessly

A Tahitian drummer sets the beat for a dancer on the beach at sunrise.

creaking ship, no wonder de Bougainville and his crew thought they had found Paradise!

In his great novel of the sea, *Moby-Dick*, published in 1851, American writer Herman Melville likens Tahiti to an oasis of perfect peace in a hostile and frightening world:

"For as this appalling ocean surrounds the verdant land, so in the soul of man there lies one insular Tahiti, full of peace and joy, but encompassed by all the horrors of the half known life. God keep thee! Push not off from that isle, thou canst never return!"

To Melville, this island of tranquillity exists not only on a map, but within the human soul. This is an important point to remember in understanding the appeal of Tahiti, both then and now.

To be sure, the island *was* far from "civilization"—very far. Even today it remains geographically remote—the nearest continent, Australia, is around 4,000 miles (6,400 kilometers) away. When traveling by plane, rather than by old-fashioned clipper ship, it is still an eight-hour flight. The Americas are about the same distance away, in the other direction. Tahiti's climate is delightful all year round, and the undeveloped parts of the landscape are beautiful. So, of course there's plenty of good reason to love this island.

In fact, Tahiti is just one of thousands of islands in the South Pacific Ocean. It's the second-largest and most populated of the 118 islands that make up the country of French Polynesia. The autonomous, but not-quite-independent, country is "French" because the region still officially belongs to France, which claimed it in the nineteenth century; and "Polynesia" because it is a subset of a larger group of more than one thousand islands called Polynesia. *Polynesia* is a term derived from the ancient Greek for "many

islands," and, coined in 1756 by a French explorer, it originally meant all of the Pacific Islands. Although Tahiti itself is just one island, it's not unusual for the entire region to be referred to as the "Tahitian Islands." This book focuses on both Tahiti and greater French Polynesia.

Probably the one man who did the most to invent the "myth" of the Tahitian paradise was Paul Gauguin. A French painter who famously fled Europe—and his own failures there—for Tahiti in 1891, he created his own vision of the "savage" life. Through his writings, and especially in his paintings, he portrayed the idyll he had hoped to find, his own imaginary Eden. The truth was more mundane. Though Gauguin's paintings are celebrated today as great art, art lovers now know these exotic scenes, with their primal colors and mystical sensibility, are romanticized fantasies, not depictions of real life on Tahiti, then or now.

Tahitian Women, by Paul Gauguin, 1891, is painted in a style called "primitivism," a Western art movement that borrows visual forms from non-Western or prehistoric peoples in a naive or folk art style.

Tahiti was, and to some extent still is, a colonized land. Its people were subject to all the usual miseries common to colonial oppression and exploitation, including the destruction of their own culture, language, religion, and heritage. By Gauguin's time, they were already well immersed in Western culture, having been forbidden their own. In the later twentieth century, they were exposed to the effects of France's nuclear testing on a neighboring archipelago over a period of three decades.

Tourism brochures tap into the myth of Tahiti as an exotic paradise, and understandably so. Tourism is Tahiti's most important industry and a large majority of the residents depend on it in one way or another for their livelihoods. By tweaking the old vision's erotic undertone, the industry now advertises Tahiti as a honeymoon destination. For example, the Frommer's travel guide says, "Whether you're on your honeymoon or not, French Polynesia is a marvelous place for romantic escapes. After all, romance and the islands have gone hand-in-hand since the young women of Tahiti gave rousing, bare-breasted welcomes to the 18th-century European explorers."

Well, that's the fantasy. Vacationers are, by definition, looking to "vacate" the reality of their everyday lives, and one way to do that is to indulge in a few days or weeks of idyllic experience. Therefore, harkening back to Melville's metaphor, Tahiti can guide the seeker to that island of perfect peace within the soul. However, the reality of Tahiti today is much more complex, and it's important not to confuse the fantasy with a true understanding of the people and their culture.

In 2014, some 181,000 tourists arrived in Tahiti; 44 percent of them from North America. But that number is down from a high of 260,000 in the year 2000. The French Polynesian Ministry of Tourism would like to push that number higher. To that end, it is working to "rebrand" Tahiti for the twenty-first century. One way it hopes to accomplish this is through its "Smart Tourism" initiative. The appeal of primitivism might have worked for Gauguin more than a century ago, but today's visitors want a total high-tech, digital experience. Upgrading and expanding the Wi-Fi cloud across the islands is a major goal.

Another goal is a focus on "authenticity," which, interestingly, is the opposite of fantasy. Many travelers today are curious to learn about a destination's history and cultural heritage. This trend ties into a corresponding effort on the part of the Tahitian people to reclaim their identity. French Polynesia enjoys more autonomy now than it has at any other time under French rule. The question citizens are grappling with now is whether to push for full independence or to retain their French citizenship. Even within the same political parties, Tahitian politicians disagree. Whether France would grant full independence and how that would affect the Tahitian economy is yet another question.

Women sell their wares at the Papeete craft and food market.

Naturally, Tahiti is not the same island it was two hundred years ago. The population is more diverse, with a large number of people of mixed Polynesian and European ethnicity, and a significant minority of Chinese background. Even for the most ardent supporters of Tahiti's heritage revival, today's way of life is so drenched in European and American culture that "authenticity" is a constant struggle against the current.

The struggle may pay off, however, not only in terms of personal and national identity but as a selling point as well. Tahiti's official tourism website reflects this in its advertising appeal—"Immersed in a world of majestic mountain peaks, turquoise waters and white-sand beaches, visitors to our islands create memories through authentic experiences that cannot be found anywhere else in the world. For centuries, the Tahitian people have referred to this as 'Mana.' Mana is a life force and spirit that surrounds and connects all living things. You can see it. Touch it. Taste it. Feel it."

GEOGRAPHY

North Pacific Ocean

South Pacific Ocean

HAWAIIAN ISLANDS (U.S.)

Kauai
Oahu
Honolulu
Maui
Hawaii

Wake Island (U.S.)

Johnston Atoll (U.S.)

Kingman Reef (U.S.)

Palmyra Atoll

Kirimati (Christmas Island) (KIRIBATI)

MARSHALL ISLANDS
Majuro

Tarawa

KIRIBATI (GILBERT ISLANDS)

Banaba

Howland Island (U.S.)

Baker Island (U.S.)

Jarvis Island (U.S.)

KIRIBATI

LINE ISLANDS

ÎLES MARQUISES

RAWAKI (PHOENIX ISLANDS)

Tokelau (N.Z.)

Funafuti
TUVALU

Swains Island

SANTA CRUZ ISLANDS

Rotuma

Wallis and Futuna (FRANCE)

Mata-Utu

SAMOA
Apia

Pago Pago

American Samoa (U.S.)

Cook Islands (N.Z.)

ARCHIPEL DES TUAMOTU

SOCIETY ISLANDS

Papeete
Tahiti

VANUATU
Port-Vila

FIJI
Suva

Vanua Levu

Viti Levu

Alofi

Niue (N.Z.)

Avarua

French Polynesia (FRANCE)

Mururoa

ÎLES GAMBIER

Noumea

Ceva-i-Ra

TONGA
Nuku'Alofa

Minerva Reefs

ÎLES TUBUAI

Adams
Pitcairn (U.K.)

Kingston
Norfolk Island (AUSTRALIA)

KERMADEC ISLANDS (N.Z.)

North Island
Auckland
Hamilton
Tauranga

NEW ZEALAND

Palmerston North
Hastings

Wellington

Christchurch

South Island

Dunedin

CHATHAM ISLANDS (N.Z.)

The islands of the South Pacific Ocean, including Tahiti, are unofficially called the "South Sea Islands."

1

TAHITI IS A SMALL ISLAND IN THE South Pacific Ocean, thousands of miles from any large mainland, about half way between South American and Australia. That description makes it sound quite isolated—and it is—but it's not out there in the vast Pacific all alone. Tahiti is the largest of 118 islands that make up French Polynesia, a scattering of five island groups, or archipelagos. These are spread over a large region, a total area of 1,545,007 square miles (4,001,550 sq km), but the islands themselves are quite small, with a combined land area of only 1,609 square miles (4,167 sq km).

French Polynesia's five archipelagos are the Society Islands, the Austral Islands, the Tuamotu Islands, the Gambier Islands, and the Marquesas Islands. The Society Islands are further divided into the Windward Islands and the Leeward Islands. Tahiti is part of the Windward group. It's the commercial, cultural, government, and social center of French Polynesia, where most of the population lives. Other important islands are Mo'orea, Huahine, and Raiatea.

The islands of French Polynesia are spread over an expanse of ocean about half the size of the United States mainland. Their total land area, however, is just slightly less than one third the size of Connecticut.

The Pacific Ocean—particularly the South Pacific—is dotted with thousands of islands, many of which, like Tahiti, are quite small. There are so many Pacific islands, in fact, that no one is certain just how many exist; most geographers estimate there are about 27,500.

Tahiti is just one tiny "star" in the 118-island "constellation" of French Polynesia, which, in turn, is a part of Polynesia—a sort of oceanic "Milky Way" of more than one thousand islands. This roughly triangular-shaped region includes Hawaii, Easter Island, and New Zealand in addition to French Polynesia and numerous other islands. The term Polynesia *is sometimes used more as a cultural descriptor than a geographical one.*

Nevertheless, Polynesia, along with Micronesia and Melanesia, two other vast island groups, make up a larger region yet of South Pacific islands called Oceania. Coined in 1812 by a French geographer, the name Oceania *is an ambiguous one. Sometimes, the region is said to also include* Malaysia (now called the Malay Archipelago), *which extends into the Indian Ocean. And still other times, Oceania is defined broadly as the entire island region between Southeast Asia to the Americas, including Australia.*

Yet another definition describes Oceania as a continent, though not one usually counted among Earth's seven large land masses. For geopolitical boundaries, islands are usually included with the continent nearest them, but in the case of the Pacific Islands, the nearest

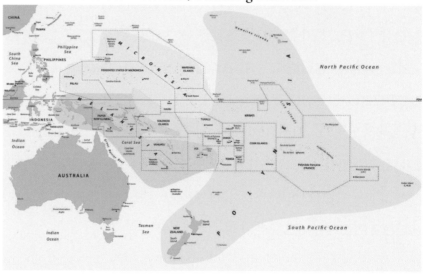

continent is not very near. Nevertheless, these far-flung islands are sometimes tied to the continent of Australia.

THE ISLAND OF TAHITI

Although Tahiti is the largest island in French Polynesia, it is only about one-third of the size of Rhode Island. However, its area of 402 square miles (1,041 sq km) accounts for about one-quarter of the total land area of French Polynesia. It is also the highest island, with its tallest mountain reaching 7,333 feet (2,235 m).

The islands of French Polynesia are of two types: volcanic islands, also called high islands, and coral islands, also called atolls. Tahiti is a high island ringed by a coral reef. It is shaped like an hourglass lying more or less horizontal. The larger section of the hourglass, Tahiti Nui (Big Tahiti), takes up the western side of the island. Papeete, the capital, is located on the northwest coast of Tahiti Nui. Most commercial and leisure activity is concentrated in the town and the area surrounding it. The airport of Faa'a is about 4 miles (6.4 km) from Papeete.

Tahiti's interior is largely mountainous.

Waterfalls are plentiful in Tahiti's lush, mountainous center.

The smaller part of Tahiti is a peninsula called Tahiti Iti (Small Tahiti) or Taiarapu. It is mostly undeveloped, and there is no road going all the way around it. The narrow neck of the hourglass is called Taravao, and it acts as a refueling center for people traveling around Tahiti. Taravao is also a dynamic town with schools, businesses, and cultural activities. Bridging Tahiti Nui and Tahiti Iti, it is larger and more developed than the neighboring districts.

Like Maui, one of the islands of Hawaii, Tahiti was formed by two ancient volcanoes, which joined at the isthmus of Taravao. The centers of both parts of Tahiti are mountainous and craggy. Steep slopes crossed by deep ravines descend to the coastal plain. Waterfalls are a common sight; Vaimahuta, near Tiarei in the northeast, is one of the most beautiful. Rainbows form above the waterfalls as the sun's rays filter through the droplets of water. In fact, there is a phrase, *Tahiti-nui-te-vai-uri-rau*, which means "Great Tahiti of the many-colored waters."

The coastal plain varies in width from a few feet (around 1 m) to more than a mile (1.6 km) at its widest in the north at Pirae and the south at Papara. Only the coastal plain is inhabited.

The northeastern coast is rugged and rocky because there is no barrier reef. Waves ride in high, pounding the shore with great intensity. Villages lie in a narrow strip between the mountains and the ocean. The Pari Coast, at the southeastern tip of the peninsula, has spectacular cliffs with a drop of nearly 1,000 feet (305 m) down to the ocean. The southern coast, on the other hand, is protected by a reef, and its sandy beaches are gently lapped by the waves. The coastal plain is broad and supports large gardens and coconut groves. All around Tahiti, the depth of the lagoon between the reef and the island varies from 25 feet (7.6 m) to 100 feet (30.5 m).

The coastline is cut here and there by deep bays. Matavai Bay is where most of the early explorers landed. All ships moored in Matavai Bay until the 1820s, when the better-protected harbor of Papeete became more popular.

Islands in the ocean are formed by underwater volcanic eruptions. As the volcano explodes, magma is pushed up above sea level, and an island emerges. At first it is shaped like a cone. After the mass has cooled down, rains erode the land over time, and valleys and mountains are carved out of the cone. Once this phase is over, the polyps (a type of microorganism) present in the sea start to form a reef, and the island gradually becomes surrounded by a ring of coral.

Over several million years, as the rains cause the island to slowly erode away, the coral reef grows higher and higher, rising to about 3–7 feet (0.9–2.1 m) above sea level. Vegetation starts to grow on this ring, and the edges become beaches. As the ring is not of the same height throughout, the parts that jut out of the sea become coral islands. These are called motu *(moh-TOO) in Tahitian. When the last*

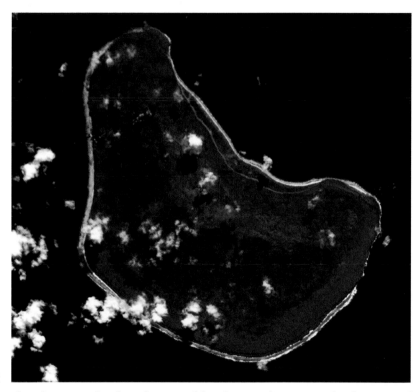

volcanic peak of the first island is completely submerged by the sea, leaving only the ring of coral islands surrounding a lagoon, an atoll is born.

"Closed" atolls have no break in the reef. The only way water is exchanged between the ocean and the lagoon is through shallow channels called hoa *(HOH-ah) in Tahitian. "Open" atolls can have one or more breaks in the reef, promoting a greater exchange of water and marine species between the ocean and the lagoon. Makatea, in the Tuamotu archipelago, is the only "raised" atoll in French Polynesia. The reef that turned into the island was wider and higher, thus forming a plateau with no lagoon.*

PEAKS AND RIVERS

There are more than one hundred rivers and streams on the island.

The centers of Tahiti Nui and Tahiti Iti are made up of several tall peaks surrounding deep depressions. The depressions, called calderas, are the former craters of the volcanoes whose explosions led to the formation of the island. The tallest mountain on Tahiti Nui is Mount Orohena. Its rounded summit rises up to 7,333 feet (2,235 m). Tahiti Iti's tallest peak is Mount Roniu at 4,341 feet (1,323 m). Altogether there are eight mountains on the island of Tahiti. One of the most intriguing outcrops is Mount Diademe, a thin rectangular blade of basalt that rises to 3,960 feet (1,207 m).

There are more than one hundred rivers and streams all over Tahiti. The longest river is Papenoo, which originates from the northern side of the caldera of Tahiti Nui. At its source, where it is spanned by the longest bridge in Tahiti, it is called Vaituoru. It then becomes Papenoo and flows 15 miles (24 km) through the Papenoo Valley down to the sea. On its way it is joined by several other rivers, finally dividing into two before reaching the sea. The widest and fastest-flowing river in Tahiti is the Vaitepiha on the peninsula.

PAPEETE

Tahiti's capital takes its name from the Papeete River, which used to flow nearby. Meaning "water basket," Papeete was nothing but swampland until Rev. James Crook, an English missionary, settled there in 1818. The missionaries of the London Missionary Society soon followed suit, and the town grew rapidly as a result. Its excellent harbor made it a place of trade

and a favorite port of call for whalers. After Tahiti was made a French colony in 1880, Papeete became the seat of the governor.

The urban spread now extends over 25 miles (40 km), from Paea in the west to Mahina in the north. The outskirting districts of Papenoo and Papara are also slowly becoming urbanized. Even the island of Moorea has become almost a suburb of Papeete, now that there are regular air and sea links between the two neighbors.

With its modern harbor facilities and the only international airport to service French Polynesia—Faa'a airport—Papeete is now a major stopover for shipping and flights across the Pacific. French Polynesia's exports are transported from the Papeete port, and a power plant supplies electricity for the island.

The town center, with warehouses and branch offices of companies, faces the harbor. Most buildings are modern and two or three stories high. Government buildings and the courts of justice are located in the administrative sector. In contrast to the rest of the town, Vaiami Hospital

Papeete lies on Tahiti's northwestern coast.

and the naval regiment are still housed in beautiful colonial buildings. Around the administrative sector is the commercial section of town, with banks and offices. To the north lies the Fare Ute industrial zone. The missionary quarter is south of the town center. Catholic and Protestant schools stand next to small houses.

The main street of Papeete is Boulevard Pomare, which curves around the harbor. It is lined with modern shopping malls, libraries, museums, and churches. The post office and the public swimming pool are also located there. In the heart of the waterfront area lies Bougainville Park, which is crowned by a massive banyan tree. This peaceful oasis features running streams and lush vegetation.

Beyond the town center is a motley collection of slums, middle-income houses, businesses, and industrial zones. Six of Tahiti's twenty-one communes (administrative districts) are adjacent to Papeete and relatively urban: Paea, Puna'auia, Faa'a, Pirae, Arue, and Mahina. The lower-income groups can be found in Faa'a, Paea, and the western side of Mahina. The higher grounds of Pirae and Puna'auia are reserved for the beautiful houses of more affluent residents.

The urban area in and around Papeete is home to more than 127,000 inhabitants, accounting for about 65 percent of the population of French Polynesia. The population of Papeete is still growing as more islanders leave their native villages to look for work in the capital. The corollary of this fast-paced growth is increasing problems of air, water, and noise pollution.

CLIMATE

Because Tahiti lies in the tropics, the climate is warm almost all year round. There are roughly two seasons: hot and rainy from November to April, with average temperatures ranging from 72 degrees Fahrenheit to 90°F (22—32° Celsius), and relatively cool and dry from May to October, with temperatures between 64°F and 72°F (18—22°C).

At high altitudes, the temperature is much lower; in the cool season, nighttime temperatures on Mount Orohena can even drop to freezing. The climate of Tahiti is tempered by cooling breezes from the sea. In the hot season, the prevailing winds are the northeast trade winds. In the cool season, it is the strong southeast trade wind, called *maraamu* (mah-rah-AH-moo), that dominates. A mountain wind called *hupe* (HOO-pay) blows down onto the coastal plains in the evening. Rainfall is erratic, with Papeete recording an average of 73 inches (185 cm) yearly. The northeast trade winds bring the most rain, and Papenoo, in the northeast, receives twice as much rain as Puna'auia on the western coast. Devastating floods are frequent in the Papenoo Valley during the rainy season.

Heavy rains in January 2017 damaged roads in the city of Faa'a.

The mountainous region in the center of the island also receives much rain. Most rain falls from December to March. Humidity is high throughout the year, reaching 98 percent during the hotter months. Tahiti also faces cyclones, which occur from January to March. Cyclone Veena in 1983 registered winds of up to 140 miles (225 km) per hour and is still remembered by Tahitians for the damage it caused.

FLORA

Tahiti used to be covered with forests of hibiscus, casuarina, rosewood, and chestnut. Along the coast, only a few pockets of these plants remain today, although wild hibiscus is still quite common on higher ground.

The plant life of Tahiti varies according to the altitude. Along the coast, aside from the pockets of forest, a variety of tropical trees grow in profusion, including coconut palms, pandanus, and almond trees. The hillsides and valleys support fruit trees such as guava, mango, lime, grapefruit, and orange. Other fruits that are planted on a large scale are pineapples, papaya, and bananas. Vanilla and coffee grow in the valleys and on the plateaus. Flowering trees include lantana, acacia, and ylang-ylang. One interesting feature of Tahitian

The tiare Tahiti (Tahitian gardenia) has a sweet, tropical fragrance.

flora is that there are no plants with thorns aside from raspberry plants and another common plant that lies flat and is easily recognized. As a result, Tahitians can walk barefoot without getting injured.

On the slopes from 1,500 feet to 2,700 feet (457—823 m) high, the vegetation consists mainly of a few trees and ferns that grow in dense clumps. Farther up, forests of hardwood trees reappear. They are called "the forest of clouds," and because of the high humidity, tree trunks are covered with epiphytes and other creepers. The strong winds blow the trunks into strange, tortuous shapes.

Tahiti's national flower is the *tiare Tahiti*, from the gardenia family. The small, white, sweet-smelling flower is used to make headdresses and garlands or simply worn behind the ear. Tahitians have a long-standing love affair with flowers. Roads are lined with hibiscus, frangipani, bougainvillea, and flame of the forest, and even the humblest house is decorated with bright flowers.

FAUNA

Land fauna in Tahiti is rather scarce. Many of the animals on the island were introduced by the first Polynesians to come to the islands. The wild pig, with a mane at the neck, a long snout, tusks, and long legs, was the first animal to be brought into Tahiti. It has become a rarity due to hunting, so it is protected from extinction by a law regulating the number of wild pigs that can be killed. Wild chickens exist in the coastal regions, and herds of wild goats roam the plateaus of Fautaua and Tuauru. The early Polynesians also brought dogs, rats, and lizards stowed away on their canoes. Europeans introduced domestic animals such as horses, cows, and cats.

Several types of fish are found in the rivers of Tahiti, including eels, jacks, sleepers, *kemeridae*, gobies, mullet, and *syngnathidae*. The most abundant are the eels, of which there are three species. Eared eels, however, have almost disappeared from Tahiti's rivers. In addition, there are four species of freshwater shrimps, a few mollusks, and some insects. The *tupa* is a land crab that digs holes and tunnels near the lagoon. There are also a number of snails, and the tiny *partula* is used for making necklaces.

The waters off the coast of Tahiti are richer in animal life. Seven hundred species of fish inhabit the lagoon, and sharks and reptiles can be found beyond the reef. Tropical fish are colorful, and some, like the grouper, can grow to substantial dimensions. Green turtles and hawksbill turtles are quite common. On rare occasions, sea snakes can be found in the water.

There are about ninety species of birds in Tahiti, most of them indigenous to French Polynesia. One of the most impressive is the tropic bird, with its two long, red tail feathers. These feathers were prized as royal emblems in ancient Tahiti. Of the land birds, the Tahitian swallow is one of the most common.

The tropic bird has distinctive long, red tail feathers.

INTERNET LINKS

https://www.britannica.com/place/French-Polynesia
The land, climate, and plant and animal life of French Polynesia are included on this site.

http://www.sea.edu/spice_atlas/tahiti_atlas/the_physical_environment_of_tahiti
This is an informative essay about Tahiti's physical environment.

http://www.worldatlas.com/webimage/countrys/oceania/tahiti.htm
This World Atlas site provides maps, photos, fast facts, and statistics about Tahiti.

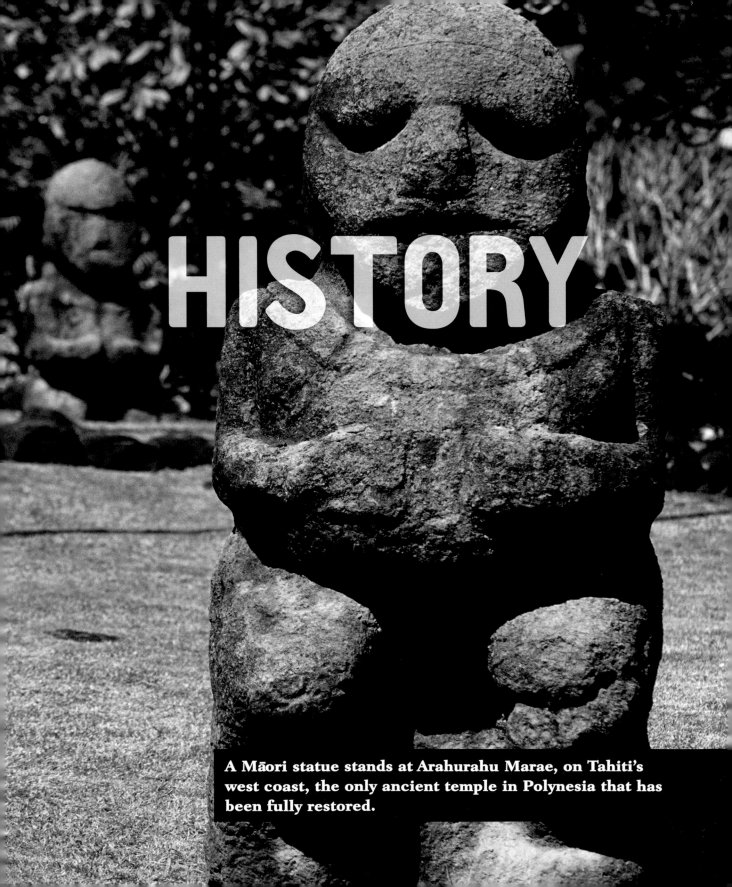

HISTORY

A Māori statue stands at Arahurahu Marae, on Tahiti's west coast, the only ancient temple in Polynesia that has been fully restored.

2

TAHITI ESSENTIALLY HAS TWO histories—before and after its discovery by European explorers. Before, the people of Tahiti led a life determined by their own culture, isolated from, and unknown to, the rest of the world. They had no writing system and did not work with metal—in fact, they did not work at all, at least not as the Europeans knew work. Apart from a few hours of fishing or collecting food, they spent most of the day engaged in leisure activities.

However, almost from the moment the island was discovered by European explorers, it attracted visitors lured by the myths of the "noble savage" and paradise on earth. European colonization and the introduction of "civilization" brought diseases and evils that did not exist there previously. The lifestyle on Tahiti was irremediably changed.

Tahiti was always described by those who visited the island in terms of what they themselves felt or perceived, never through the eyes of the local population. Even today, its rich "prediscovery" history is overshadowed by the events related to the appearance of the first European explorers. Tahitians are still perceived as a gentle people leading an idyllic lifestyle. The reality is that of a subjugated people who have long demanded political independence. Although Tahitians

"Not only are the majority of these islands of surpassing loveliness and fertility, with a delightful climate and magnificent mountain scenery, but they are inhabited by a most interesting race of people, at whose history we will briefly glance, from their heathen state when visited by Captain Cook in 1769, down to their comparatively civilised condition at the present day."

—from *The Colonies*, published 1876, London

now enjoy a greater degree of autonomy under the French government and more control over many aspects of daily life, they still do not have complete sovereignty over their destiny.

POLYNESIAN ANCESTORS

Polynesian prehistory is still very much a mystery. Who are the Polynesian people, where did they come from, and how, when—and why—did they populate the Pacific Islands, some of the most remote places on earth? The answers to these questions have largely been settled, and yet new archaeological and genetic research is challenging previous assumptions. However, no alternative theory has yet been sufficiently accepted to replace the conventional thinking.

Most Pacific Island scholars think the first people to settle in Polynesia came from Southeast Asia. Traveling east, they settled in Fiji around 1500 BCE, then in Tonga and Samoa a few centuries later. From these islands, they set sail for what is now French Polynesia around 300 CE, settling first in the Marquesas. During the next one thousand years they settled in Easter Island, Hawaii, the Society Islands, and New Zealand.

Overpopulation on one island led the Polynesians to set off in search of new islands. The first step was to make a voyage of exploration for suitable islands. Once a sufficiently large island was found, the explorers noted its direction in relation to the stars and returned home to fetch their families, animals, and plants so as to establish settlements on the new island.

The ancient Polynesians were skilled navigators. They traveled in large double-hulled canoes, using the position of the sun and the stars to direct them. They were also able to anticipate the appearance and proximity of land by noting changes in the waves.

By sailing a raft called *Kon-Tiki* from Peru to islands east of Tahiti in 1947, Swedish explorer Thor Heyerdahl tried to prove that the Polynesians could have come from South America. This theory has largely been debunked as a result of archaeological findings. However, it is almost certain that there was some form of contact, as the sweet potato, which originated in South

America, can be found in Polynesia, even if corn—the staple food of South America—does not. Historians tend to believe that if South Americans had gone on to colonize the islands, they would certainly have brought their staple food along.

In 1976 the *Hōkūle'a*, an oceangoing canoe built from ancient designs, sailed from Hawaii to Tahiti using only traditional Polynesian navigational techniques based on the stars and the swells of waves. This voyage proved beyond doubt that the ancient Polynesians were some of the greatest sailors of all time.

In 2014, the Hōkūle'a, a full scale replica of an ancient Polynesian double-hulled voyaging canoe, embarked on a three-year circumnavigation of the world.

TAHITI BEFORE THE EUROPEANS

Ancient Tahitian society was highly hierarchical. There were three distinct classes: *arii* (ah-REE-ee), or high chiefs; *raatira* (rah-AH-tee-rah), or minor chiefs and landowners; and *manahune* (mah-nah-HOO-nay), or common

When Captain Samuel Wallis landed in Tahiti in 1767, he was not searching for a tiny tropical island. Rather, he had been sailing the South Pacific in search of a large landmass that was then thought to exist south of the Equator. Although no one had yet seen this hypothetical continent, its existence was based on the theory that continental land in the Northern Hemisphere must be balanced by an equal amount of land in the Southern Hemisphere. This idea had been promulgated since the time of ancient Greece and Rome, and was generally accepted as accurate. Medieval mapmakers in Europe would draw an imaginary land in the unexplored southern part of the world where they guessed the continent might lie.

The search for Terre Australis *(Latin for "South Land") spurred Europeans to sail to these unknown southern regions, and Wallis was one of them. When he finally returned to England and reported his discovery of Tahiti, the British government in 1769 sent explorer James Cook to return to the South Pacific to find the* Terra Incognita *("Unknown Land") of the Southern Hemisphere.*

Eventually, as further exploration failed to find the hypothetical continent, the theory fell out of favor. The name Terre Australis was given to Australia when it seemed there was no other option. It wouldn't be until 1820 that Antarctica became the last region on Earth to be discovered. Terre Australis was found at last, but by then, the name Australia was firmly stuck to the land that now bears it. Antarctica's discovery also proved that the "balanced hemispheres" theory was incorrect. The Southern Hemisphere has far less land mass than the North.

people. People from the different classes did not mix with each other, and children born of the union between a chief and a commoner were killed. Men and women were segregated most of the time, especially at mealtimes, and women were not allowed to participate in religious ceremonies.

The *arii* had absolute authority over their subjects, who considered the *arii* almost godlike. The *arii* had to be physically higher than everyone else and were carried everywhere by their subjects. When they stood, their subjects had to sit down; when they were seated, others had to lie down.

The *manahune* were servants, farmers, and fishermen. They could not move out of their class unless they became priests or warriors. Between the chiefs and the commoners were the landowners. The landowners owed the same respect to the chiefs as the *manahune*, and their authority was limited to relaying orders from the chiefs to the commoners and seeing that they were carried out.

Tahiti was divided into several districts, each ruled by an *arii*. Wars frequently broke out between the tribes, and the vanquished were often taken as slaves by the victors.

EUROPEAN DISCOVERY

On June 17, 1767, Captain Samuel Wallis chanced upon the island of Tahiti during an exploratory trip. He anchored his ship, the HMS *Dolphin*, at Taiarapu in the southern part of the island. The next day he sailed farther north looking for a more pleasant anchorage and landed in Matavai Bay. Hundreds of canoes surrounded the ship, and the islanders seemed friendly at first. However, they then started pelting the crew with stones, and the Englishmen opened fire with their cannons. On June 24, Wallis took formal possession of the island for the British crown and called it King George III's Island. After a few more rounds of cannon firing, the Tahitians decided to cooperate with the invaders and supplied them with fresh water and food. The *Dolphin* left Tahiti after a few weeks, but news of the discovery did not reach England until a year later.

Two French ships, the *Etoile* and the *Boudeuse*, under the command of Louis-Antoine de Bougainville, arrived in Tahiti in April 1768. Unaware of the

This old etching illustrates Tahiti's surrender to Captain Samuel Wallis in 1767.

visit of Wallis and the English claim to the island, Bougainville claimed Tahiti for France, giving it the name of New Cythera, in reference to the birthplace of the Greek goddess of love, Aphrodite. Back in France, he promoted the idea of an idyllic land where a gentle people lived on the bounty of the land and the sea, free from the restrictions of European life. Bougainville's recollections of Tahiti were published in 1771 in a book entitled *Voyage autour du monde* ("Voyage around the world"). The book was a resounding success and spread the myth of the island paradise.

The third European associated with Tahiti was the English explorer Captain James Cook, who visited the island four times between 1769 and 1777. During his first visit, he stayed three months to observe the transit of the planet Venus across the sun. He traveled around the whole island and drew a precise map of Tahiti. With him were two botanists, Joseph Banks and Daniel Solander, who collected an enormous number of species of plants, birds, fish, and insects, which added greatly to the scientific knowledge of the time. Cook's subsequent voyages enabled him to give the world greater details of Polynesian society.

After Captain James Cook's second voyage to Tahiti, a young man named Omai, from the island of Raiatea, boarded Cook's ship and sailed to England with the expedition. Omai acted as translator on the other islands they visited and was greeted with much interest upon his arrival in England. Omai, being a curiosity, was presented to the king and introduced to the prominent members of English society. He attended balls and parties and even inspired a few successful plays. Omai returned to Tahiti with Cook in 1777, but his long absence made him feel alienated from his own people.

A painting of Omai with two English nobles by William Parry, 1775-1776.

European romantic literature of the eighteenth century glorified the concept of the "noble savage," who symbolized natural goodness untouched by civilization. However, the concept could also take on a paternalistic note, seeing the "savages" as primitive, childlike, and animalistic. Such an outlook was often used as a justification for forcing European "civilization" on people of other cultures.

At the time of Tahiti's discovery by Europeans, the local population numbered around 150,000. As they had to the native people of the Americas, the Europeans inadvertently brought diseases to which the Tahitians had no immunity—syphilis, tuberculosis, smallpox, and dysentery. By 1865, only 7,169 Tahitians remained.

MUTINY ON THE BOUNTY

In 1788, Lieutenant William Bligh came to Tahiti on board the HMS Bounty *to collect young breadfruit trees to take to the West Indies. Bligh and his crew lived among the*

Tahitians for five months, and it was with reluctance that his crew subsequently set sail for Jamaica. Partly due to Bligh's severe treatment of the crew, many men supported crewman Fletcher Christian when he masterminded a mutiny to get rid of the ship's commander and return to blissful Polynesia. Bligh was abandoned on the open sea in a small open boat with eighteen loyal men and some basic supplies. In one of

Fletcher Christian and the *Bounty* mutineers turn Lieutenant William Bligh and eighteen others adrift in this 1790 painting by Robert Dodd.

the most impressive open-boat journeys in history, Bligh subsequently sailed 3,600 miles (5,794 km) to the Dutch Indies (Indonesia), suffering only one casualty on the way.

The mutineers first tried to settle on the Austral Islands but had to withdraw to Tahiti in the face of the inhabitants' hostility. Sixteen of them decided to stay in Tahiti. Christian, the rest of the crew, and a group of Tahitians sailed the Bounty *to the uninhabited island of Pitcairn, where they burned the ship and founded the island's first settlement. The mutineers who settled in Tahiti were recaptured by a contingent on the HMS* Pandora *less than two years later. Four drowned in a shipwreck on the return trip, and the survivors were court-martialed in England. Three of the men were hanged.*

The Bounty *drama inspired three movies, made in 1935, 1962, and 1984. To this day, most of the fifty residents of Pitcairn Island are descendants of the* Bounty *mutineers and the Tahitians who accompanied them.*

MISSIONARIES AND COLONIAL POLITICS

Thirty years after the island was discovered by Europeans, a shipload of missionaries from the London Missionary Society arrived in Tahiti to convert the "heathens" from their "idolatrous ways." It took them fifteen years to make their first convert, King Pomare II, who realized that the missionaries could be very useful to his rule and that British commerce was important for the island. The Pomare clan had gained access to firearms through their association with the European explorers, enabling them to gain supremacy over the whole island and to establish Pomare I as the first king of Tahiti in 1790. After the conversion of Pomare II in 1812, all the other Tahitians followed suit, and the ancient Polynesian religion disappeared forever.

King Pomare II

For nearly forty years the Protestant missionaries enjoyed tremendous success in Tahiti. When Catholic missionaries arrived in 1835 with the intention of establishing their own mission (having failed in a brief attempt in 1774), the Protestants used their influence over the reigning monarch, Queen Pomare IV, to send them away.

In 1837 George Pritchard, a Protestant missionary, became the English consul. He encouraged Queen Pomare to ask the British to make Tahiti a protectorate of the English crown. In 1842 French admiral Abel Dupetit-Thouars arrived in Tahiti during the absence of both the English consul and the queen. With the help of the French consul, he organized the pro-French district chiefs to sign a demand for French protection. The French began to install themselves very firmly on the island, and after a series of threats Queen Pomare was forced to ratify the demand for a protectorate. On September 9, 1842, Tahiti was proclaimed a French protectorate. A government was established that consisted of the royal commissioner, a military governor, and the captain of the port of Papeete.

THE FRENCH-TAHITIAN WAR

Tahiti is proclaimed a protectorate of France in 1842 in this scene by the French illustrator Max Radiguet.

After Tahiti officially became a protectorate of the French government, a protectorate flag was hoisted above Queen Pomare's palace, in place of her personal flag. Unhappy with this action, she protested to the king of France and looked to Britain for protection by taking refuge on the HMS *Basilisk*, an English ship anchored in the Papeete Harbor. This was the signal the population was waiting for; they immediately started a rebellion against the French invaders. Tahitian chiefs often took advantage of English and French disagreements by making alliances to further their own political aspirations and power struggles. To this end, the powerful rival chief Tati of Papara sided with the French in the hopes of gaining influence and overthrowing Pomare.

The first skirmishes took place in Taravao in March 1844. The following month, Governor Armand-Joseph Bruat engaged four hundred men to carry out a bloody battle on Mahaena beach. The Tahitians lost 102 men and retreated to the Punaruu and Papenoo Valleys to carry out guerrilla attacks on the French forces. The fighting spread to the other islands, and the Polynesians experienced some success in January 1846 in Huahine, prompting them to attack Papeete, where they were defeated. The French-Tahitian War lasted nearly three years, ending when the French troops launched a decisive attack on Fautaua fort in December 1846. Queen Pomare agreed to accept the protectorate over Tahiti and Moorea on January 7, 1847.

FRENCH OCEANIA

At the time of the protectorate, the central structure of Tahitian administration was composed of the royal court, the assembly, and the district councils. French authority was represented by the governor, assisted by various officers and civil servants. In 1880, Tahiti became a full-fledged French colony. In 1885 Tahiti and the other islands in the archipelago became the Établissements Français de l'Océanie (the French Colony of Oceania, or French Oceania).

This period was marked by the arrival of the French and other colonizers. The French settlers were mainly soldiers and sailors who decided to stay on after demobilization. Having no income of their own, they tried their hand at agriculture, cultivating the lands of their Tahitian wives without much success. The English, the Americans, and the Germans were more successful because they came from a wealthier background. Those who married into the local aristocracy gained access to much land and capital. Thus were started the wealthy families who still rule the world of commerce in Tahiti: the Salmons, the Laharragues, the Branders, and the Horts.

The Chinese were brought in as coolies to work in the cotton fields at Atimaono in the mid-1800s. Other immigrants came from Melanesia, the Gilbert Islands (now called Kiribati), Atiu, and Easter Island.

INTERNAL AUTONOMY

Tahiti was largely neglected by France at the beginning of the twentieth century, and life there was harsh. Diseases and cyclones caused great destruction. However, with the opening of the Panama Canal in 1914, Tahiti became a port of call between Australia and the United States, and subsidies from the Colonial Office started to pour in. When World War I broke out, Tahiti sent a small contingent of volunteers for France.

After World War II, during which the Tahitian battalion earned honors at Bir Hakeim in North Africa, universal suffrage was granted to French Oceania in 1945, and all residents of the colony were granted French citizenship. In 1947, a World War I volunteer, Pouvanaa a Oopa, created the Pouvanaa Committee to oppose the arrival of additional civil servants from France. From then on, there were more demands for autonomy in Tahiti. On July 27, 1957, French Oceania changed from a colony to a territory and became known as French Polynesia. After General Charles de Gaulle became president of France in 1958, a referendum was held to allow Tahitians to

Despite vocal protests from the local population, the Centre d'Expérimentation du Pacifique (CEP)—Center for Experimentation in the Pacific—was set up in 1963 on the atolls of Moruroa and Fangataufa, about 750 miles (1,207 km) from Tahiti. French military personnel were stationed in large numbers in Tahiti, and the French military presence is still strongly felt in the country. The CEP was headquartered at Pirae, just east of Papeete, with a major support base opposite the yacht club at Arue.

The first bomb was detonated at Moruroa on July 2, 1966. Initially nuclear testing took place in the atmosphere, but in 1974, after forty-four atmospheric explosions and following strong international protests, the CEP decided to switch to underground tests. In total, more than 190 nuclear devices were detonated.

In 1995, newly elected French president Jacques Chirac unleashed a storm of protests worldwide when the French government announced that it would resume nuclear testing in French Polynesia after having unofficially discontinued testing for three years. Rioting broke out in Papeete, the passenger terminal at the Faa'a airport was set on fire, and troops were called in from other territories to quell the unrest. Among the demonstrators were young unemployed Tahitians, supporters of Tahiti's independence, and antinuclear activists from various Pacific Rim countries. In the face of such strong sentiment, the French government reduced the number of devices to be detonated from eight to six and announced that those were the last tests. The program effectively ended in 1996.

One of the highest-profile incidents was the sinking of the Rainbow Warrior *in 1985. The Greenpeace vessel was docked in Auckland Harbor in New Zealand while on its way to French Polynesia with a flotilla of yachts to protest the nuclear program when it was sunk by a group of French secret agents who had infiltrated the organization. The sinking caused a major international scandal, and two agents were sentenced to prison by a New Zealand court. In 2005, it was revealed that the operation had been personally sanctioned by the highest authorities in France, including then-president François Mitterand himself.*

From the French political point of view, nuclear testing was necessary to maintain France's position as a world political and military power. The authorities dismissed the fears of Pacific Rim nations and maintained that nuclear test sites in Russia are actually closer to Paris than Moruroa is to its nearest neighbor. The French government, however, has never allowed any proper study to be conducted on the test atolls, maintaining a ban on any outside investigations of the sites that had been rigorously enforced since 1966. The French defense ministry is still in charge of the two atolls.

In 1998, France ratified the Comprehensive Nuclear-Test-Ban Treaty of 1996, a multilateral treaty adopted by the United Nations General Assembly that bans all nuclear explosions, for both civilian and military purposes in all environments.

In 2014, French Polynesia's assembly adopted a resolution asking France to pay nearly $1 billion in compensation for the environmental damage caused by its nuclear weapons tests. However, the supporters of President Edouard Fritch boycotted the vote, essentially shutting it down.

decide whether they wanted to remain French. Nearly two-thirds of the electorate were in favor of staying with the French commonwealth.

NUCLEAR TESTING

In 1963, France moved its nuclear program from Algeria—which had by then acquired independence—to French Polynesia. Subsequently the government of France conducted nearly two hundred nuclear tests on the islands of Moruroa and Fangataufa between 1966 and 1996. This program had wide-ranging repercussions on Tahitian society that are still being felt today, in ecological, health, and economic terms.

With the setting up of the Center for Experimentation in the Pacific (CEP) and the arrival of its attendant problems, more and more Tahitians called out for greater autonomy. In 1977, Tahiti was granted a new statute, giving the islanders slightly more say in its management. In 1984, full internal autonomy came into effect, and twenty years later, in 2004, the territory acquired more self-governing powers when it was officially designated as a *pays d'outre-mer* ("overseas country").

VOICES FOR INDEPENDENCE

With the election of Oscar Temaru to the French Polynesian presidency in 2004, French Polynesia had, for the first time in its history, a proindependence majority in parliament. The proindependence movement gained momentum after 1996 when, with the cessation of nuclear testing, the country's main source of income, the military, was suddenly cut off, resulting in widespread unemployment.

A former officer in the French navy, Temaru started his political career as an antinuclear activist. In May 2004, at the head of a five-party coalition, he was elected president of French Polynesia, only to be ousted in October of the same year by political maneuvering among his rivals. Following a popular outcry, by-elections were held in February 2005, and Temaru was reinstated as president in March 2005.

Although Temaru campaigned on a pro-independence platform, he also pledged that outright independence was not for the immediate future. In fact, only 20 percent of the local population favors full independence, although the majority of the parties in the governing coalition are pro-autonomy. The new government's program included an increase in minimum wages, workdays that do not start before 9 a.m., an improvement in social services, political decentralization, education reform, and a revision of the autonomy statute.

In the 2013 election, the pendulum swung the other way and the pro-autonomy, anti-independence Popular Rally Party gained the majority, with Edward Fritch becoming president in September 2014.

http://www.captcook-ne.co.uk/ccne/themes/omai.htm
This page on the Captain Cook Museum site tells the story of Omai with images and news clippings.

http://www.government.pn/index.php
This official site of the Pitcairn Islands government provides an in-depth history of this extraordinary place.

http://www.infoplease.com/spot/pitcairn.html
The story of the mutiny on the *Bounty* and the settlement of Pitcairn Island is related on this page.

http://www.lonelyplanet.com/tahiti-and-french-polynesia/history
Lonely Planet provides an overview of Tahiti's history.

https://www.nytimes.com/2016/11/02/science/south-pacific-islands-migration.html?_r=0
This short article posits a theory about human migration to the South Pacific Islands.

http://www.radionz.co.nz/international/pacific-news/307804/the-battle-continues,-50-years-after-first-test-at-mururoa
This 2016 Radio New Zealand article discusses the lasting effects of the nuclear testing in French Polynesia.

http://www.tahiti.com/travel/about-tahiti
This travel site presents the history of Tahiti in an illustrated timeline.

GOVERNMENT

Gaston Flosse, the five-term president of French Polynesia, attends a celebration marking the thirtieth anniversary of autonomy in June 2014.

3

FRENCH POLYNESIA HAS ITS OWN president, but it's not an independent country. The president of France has final jurisdiction over the president of French Polynesia. It's a confusing situation, to be sure. Some French Polynesians are content with this arrangement, but many are not.

Since 2003, French Polynesia has enjoyed the status of being a *collectivité d'outre-mer de la République française (COM)*, an "overseas collectivity of the French Republic." This designation is one of several statuses that France has assigned to its eleven populated overseas departments and territories. A statutory law of February 27, 2004, gave French Polynesia the further designation of *pays d'outre-mer au sein de la République (POM)*, an "overseas country inside the Republic"—which is basically a different name for the same status. This means French Polynesia is essentially a country within a country, not geographically but legally. As such, it enjoys a greater degree of autonomy now than it previously had under French rule. The assembly of French Polynesia, based in Tahiti, is in charge of most of the government, with France's influence limited to providing subsidies, education, and security.

However, the constitution of France remains the supreme law of the land. Tahitians are French citizens, vote in French elections, and are represented in the French Parliament. Pro-independence movements have made appeals to the United Nations Special Committee of Twenty-four, a group that helps colonies achieve independence. It lists French

One of the most beautiful buildings in the capital city of French Polynesia is the Papeete City Hall. Opened in 1990, it was constructed in the style of the nineteenth-century Royal Palace, which occupied the same spot before it was razed in the 1960s.

The Parliament building of French Polynesia is located in Papeete.

Polynesia as one of the world's Non-Self-Governing Territories. In 2015, the UN General Assembly adopted a resolution reaffirming the "inalienable right of the people of French Polynesia to self determination."

THE ASSEMBLY

Tahiti, in common with the rest of French Polynesia, is governed by a territorial government made up of a president, a vice president, and twenty-two ministers, who are in charge of the daily running of the territory. The president is elected by the assembly of French Polynesia, which also ratifies the president's choice of ministers.

Legislative power is in the hands of the fifty-seven members of the assembly, who are elected for a period of five years. The territory is divided into districts, with thirty-seven seats going to the Windward Islands (including Tahiti and Moorea), eight to the Leeward Islands, three to the Gambier Islands and the Tuamotu-East, three to the Tuamotu-West, three to the Austral Islands, and three to the Marquesas. Because of the electoral system, one vote in the Tuamotus has the weight of three in Tahiti. The assembly's primary function is to vote on the budget, but it can also dismiss the government through a motion of censure.

Outside of the two annual assembly sessions, a permanent commission is in place. In addition, the Economic and Social Committee brings together representatives from the various professions and establishes yearly reports.

The Tahitian flag, composed of one horizontal white stripe between two red stripes, disappeared after the death of Pomare V, the last king of Tahiti. It was reinstated in 1975 alongside the French national flag. In 1984, when the territory attained internal autonomy, the French government recognized the Tahitians' right to determine the symbols expressing the personality of their nation, and this was how the current flag came about. A stylized canoe in red floating above a blue sea with yellow rays of sun at the back was added to the middle of the previous flag. Today this flag represents the whole of French Polynesia and is flown side by side with the French tricolor.

FRANCE AND TAHITI

France is represented in the territory by a high commissioner. Assisted by a secretary-general, the high commissioner is in charge of the civil service, monetary policy, the national police, foreign affairs, immigration, defense, justice, and tertiary education. Despite the changes made by the statute of 2004, the high commissioner still wields considerable power and can dissolve the Territorial Assembly or refer its decisions to an administrative tribunal. The high commissioner can also impose a state of emergency if necessary.

French Polynesia is represented in Paris by two elected deputies in the French national assembly, two senators in the Franch Senate, and a social and economic councilor.

TROUBLE IN PARADISE

Even idyllic islands aren't immune from the sleazy side of politics. In September 2014, Edouard Fritch became president of French Polynesia after his predecessor, long-time politician Gaston Flosse, was convicted of corruption and forced to resign.

Edouard FRITCH

Flosse, who had served as president on five separate occasions since his first term in 1984, also led the pro-autonomy, anti-independence Popular Rally party for more than twenty years. This is the preferred political party of most of the non-Polynesian people in French Polynesia. Over his long political career, Flosse also served in a variety of other governmental capacities, including being elected to the French Senate several times.

In 2014, Flosse was found guilty of creating a vast network of nonexistent jobs to support his political party. It became one of the biggest cases of its kind in French legal history. He was sentenced to a four-year suspended jail term, a large fine, and banned from public office for three years. He tried but failed to get a pardon from French President Francois Hollande. The conviction was upheld by France's highest court.

As of 2015, Flosse continued to serve as the head of his political party. Fritch, while also a member of the same party, opposed Flosse, which created a rift in the party.

Because Tahitians are granted full French citizenship, all persons aged eighteen and older are allowed to take part in national as well as local elections. Tahitians vote for members of the Territorial Assembly and for their representatives in the French national assembly and senate. They also participate in elections for the European parliament. French civil servants and soldiers can vote in local elections (for the municipal councils and the Territorial Assembly) the day they arrive in the territory,

and the conservative pro-French parties in the Territorial Assembly are propped up mainly by votes from French expatriates working in Tahiti.

At one time, it was the law that all men between the ages of eighteen and thirty-five—in Tahiti as in France—had to serve one year of active duty in the army, the navy, or the air force. Those who were not fit for military service had to serve two years of public service work or were deployed in other sectors of the government. In fact, many of the French civil servants in Tahiti used to be young Frenchmen in military service.

LOCAL GOVERNMENT

French Polynesia is divided into forty-eight communes, with twelve in Tahiti. The communes in the peninsula and the eastern half of Tahiti Nui are gathered into four groups of "associated communes." Each commune is managed by an elected municipal council, which chooses a mayor from its ranks. There are more than nine hundred municipal councilors throughout French Polynesia,

The first seeds of nationalism were sown by Pouvanaa a Oopa, an outspoken World War I hero from Huahine. In 1947 he founded the Pouvanaa Committee, which became the Rassemblement Démocratique des Populations Tahitiennes (Tahitian Democratic Group, or RDPT) in 1949. The RDPT was opposed to further deployment of French civil servants in Tahiti and wanted the country to move gradually toward independence. Pouvanaa's election to the French Chamber of Deputies in 1949 and to the vice presidency of the Government Council in 1957 afforded him a great opportunity to spread his separatist message among the population of Tahiti.

However, after he opposed General Charles de Gaulle during the constitutional referendum of 1958, Pouvanaa was arrested on trumped-up charges of arson, sentenced to jail, and exiled from Tahiti. Pouvanaa was not freed until 1968, well after the nuclear-testing facilities were established. In a powerful political comeback, he was elected to the French senate in 1971 and remained a senator until his death in 1977. Tahitians refer to him as te metua, *"the father," as he is credited as being the father of Tahitian nationalism. His statue stands outside the Territorial Assembly.*

Pouvanaa's legacy has been the creation of several pro-independence political parties. However, Tahitian politics is full of nuances. Most parties are nationalistic, but not all favor full independence. Those that actively call for immediate independence from France are the Polynesian Liberation Front, the Let the People Take the Power Party, and the Free Tahitians' Party. Most politicians, however, favor a more moderate form of independence, in which Tahiti could enjoy complete self-government without severing its ties with France.

Nationalism is strongest on the island of Tahiti and weakest in the Tuamotu Islands and the Marquesas, which are heavily dependent on French aid. Much of the rioting that took place in Papeete in September 1995 following France's resumption of nuclear testing in the Pacific was blamed on separatists trying to publicize their cause to the rest of the world. However, it is strategically important for France to maintain a colony in the Asia-Pacific region, where other countries still have military bases. Because France does not want to lose this foothold, it is unwilling to grant full independence to Tahiti or the rest of French Polynesia.

elected by majority vote for a period of six years. The population size of each commune determines how many councilors it is entitled to elect.

Each archipelago is run by an administrator, usually a French civil servant, appointed by the state. He or she has almost complete control over the elected municipal councils. The administrators of the Windward, Tuamotu-Gambier, and Austral Islands are based in Papeete.

Local government is responsible for public hygiene, social services, and energy. Since French Polynesia achieved internal autonomy it has also been responsible for the local police. One of the duties of the mayor is to solemnize marriages.

The City Hall Building in Papeete is one of Tahiti's best examples of nineteenth-century French colonial architecture.

INTERNET LINKS

https://www.cia.gov/library/publications/the-world-factbook/geos/fp.html
CIA World Factbook. This site provides reliable, up-to-date information about the government of French Polynesia.

http://www.radionz.co.nz/international/pacific-news/322220/pouvanaa-a-oopa-death-marked-in-french-polynesia
This Radio New Zealand article notes continuing efforts to legally clear Pouvanaa a Oopa's name.

ECONOMY

Tourists swim in the clear waters of Moorea Island 12 miles (19 km) off the northwestern coast of Tahiti.

TOURISM IS MORE THAN THE backbone of the Tahitian economy; it's nearly the entire body. About 80 percent of Tahitians earn their living working in the tourism sector in one way or another.

Tahitian currency, the French Pacific franc.

4

Unlike most of the other French overseas departments, Tahiti does not use the euro as legal tender. The currency in use in the whole of French Polynesia as well as in New Caledonia is the French Pacific franc (XPF). As it is linked to the euro, the currency is fairly stable. Pacific franc bills carry pictures of sailboats, flowers, coconut trees, and Polynesian people.

Life on Tahiti began to change drastically in the 1960s. That was when France built the island's first international airport and set up the Centre d'Expérimentation du Pacifique (CEP) (Pacific Experimentation Center) to conduct nuclear tests. Large numbers of Westerners arrived in the islands to live and work. Suddenly Tahiti was thrust into the modern world of consumerism. Instead of cultivating their own crops and fishing for their food, Tahitians became wage earners and had to depend on others to supply their dietary needs. Thousands were employed by the CEP and other government bodies.

With the end of nuclear testing in 1996, this source of income suddenly stopped, replaced by a yearly economic development transfer of 18 billion French Pacific francs (US$189.5 million). Known by its acronym of DGDE, this money is paid by France directly into the French Polynesian budget to compensate the country for the customs taxes that it no longer receives from imported material connected with the nuclear testing operations.

Inevitably, with economic activity becoming far more complex and subject to the vagaries of the global economy, unemployment continues to rise. Those who became jobless after 1996 have been joined by immigrants from the outer islands as well as by young Tahitians leaving school with few qualifications. These jobless or occasional workers account for the growing slums on the outskirts of Papeete.

Subsistence agriculture is practiced mainly in the smaller islands, while most residents of Tahiti lead an urban lifestyle, working in factories and offices and spending their free time shopping, watching movies, and having fun with their friends.

GOVERNMENT SPENDING

Tahiti is heavily dependent on French government spending. At the departure of the French military upon the closure of the CEP, the French government pledged to maintain financial aid for civil activities in Tahiti in order to support the territory in fundamentally transforming its economy. The funding was originally conceived as a limited subsidy to help the territory readjust its economy, which was overly dependent on military spending. However, the subsidy has since been converted into an annual transfer.

In 2016, France said it planned to give French Polynesia an additional $10 million beginning the following year as part of its nuclear compensation payment. According to the High Commission, the French budget will allot French Polynesia $100 million as a so-called autonomy fund.

All residents of Tahiti, including French expatriates, pay a "solidarity tax" in lieu of personal income tax. In 1998 the government embarked on a vast reform of the taxation system, with the introduction of value-added tax (VAT), the abolition of import duties, and the lowering of customs duties in accordance with World Trade Organization directives. With the presence of the highly paid and free-spending French civil servants, the cost of living in Tahiti is very high, and even with the help of unemployment and social-security benefits, many Tahitians find it difficult to make ends meet.

A farmer spreads coconut kernels to dry. They will be used to make a soothing skin and hair product called Tahitian monoi, a scented oil made from soaking tiare flowers in coconut oil.

AGRICULTURE

Since much of Tahiti's interior is mountainous, very little land is devoted to agriculture. Agricultural activity takes place mainly in four areas: Papara commune, Teva I Uta commune, the isthmus and plateau of Taravao, and the east coast. With the use of modern technology, agriculture in these areas is practiced on an intensive basis. Even so, this sector now employs 13 percent of the French Polynesian workforce but accounts for only 2.5 percent of the territory's total output.

Nearly half of the lowlands of Papara are under cultivation. The commune produces vegetables, flowers, pork, and poultry. The neighboring commune of Teva I Uta specializes in vegetable production and cattle rearing. Cattle are

raised on coconut plantations, and the coconut plantations of Teva I Uta are the largest in Tahiti. However, many of the coconut trees are more than one hundred years old, and Tahiti accounts for only a small percentage of the territory's production of copra (the dried white flesh of the coconut). Most of the commune's agricultural activity is concentrated in the coastal areas of Mataiea and Papeari. Dairy cattle are reared in Taravao, where citrus fruits—oranges in particular—and honey are also produced. The east coast of Tahiti is devoted mostly to subsistence farming, but flowers (anthuriums, *opuhi*, and orchids) are grown on a large scale in the districts of Mahaena and Tiarei.

Despite the use of modern farming methods and machinery, agricultural production does not satisfy local demand. Many products are imported from other islands or other countries—Australia and New Zealand in particular. To make the situation worse, much of the land under cultivation is being taken over by residential development, especially in Papara, Mahaena, and Tiarei.

A man extracts a pearl at an oyster farm workshop in Tahiti.

TRADE

Tahiti has a severe imbalance in trade, with exports equaling only 20 percent of its imports. Nearly half of all imports come from France, which has imposed a series of self-favoring restrictions. Imports include food, fuel, building materials, consumer goods, and automobiles. The main exports are copra, which is crushed into coconut oil and animal feed in a mill in Papeete, and cultured pearls. Copra and pearls are not produced on the island of Tahiti itself but in the Tuamotus and other outer islands. Exports of fish have steadily risen in the past few years, and this sector has been identified by the government as an important area of growth. Tahiti's main trading partners, apart from France, are the United States, Australia, New Zealand, and other islands in the Pacific.

BLACK PEARLS

The black pearl industry is the second-largest source of revenue for French Polynesia, after tourism. Black pearls are raised in more than sixty-five cooperatives and farms in the Tuamotu and Gambier Islands, where the Pinctada margaritifera (mother-of-pearl) oyster abounds.

To produce a pearl, a farmer introduces an implant (a tiny spherical object) into the oyster, which coats it with mother-of-pearl secretion. This process takes two years. Implantation is performed almost exclusively by Japanese specialists, although more Tahitians are becoming proficient at it. After implantation, the oysters are returned to the sea tied to long ropes. As many as twenty thousand oysters are farmed at one time. But the success rate is very low: only 30–50 percent of the oysters actually produce a pearl.

Several types of pearls are harvested. Keshis are deformed pearls composed exclusively of mother-of-pearl. They occur when the implant is rejected by the oyster after it has been returned to the sea. Baroque pearls have imperfections in shape. Perfect pearls are smooth and round, with a metallic green-gray or blue-gray color. Only 3 percent of the harvest is perfect.

The cooperatives sell their pearls at an auction in Papeete every October. Local jewelers vie with Japanese buyers at these events, with more than forty thousand black pearls changing hands. Private farms sell their production through independent dealers or plush retail outlets in Papeete.

TOURISM

Tourism started in earnest with the opening of Tahiti's Faa'a International Airport in 1961. The airport spurred a boom in hotel construction, and small, interisland air services began to the outer islands of Moorea and Bora Bora, which boosted tourism to those locations as well. Today tourism is the main revenue sector of French Polynesia's economy. In 2015, some 183,800 tourists visited the Tahitian islands, of which 63,913 were US citizens.

Some Australian, Asian, and US tourists regard Tahiti as a stopover destination, spending a couple of days in Papeete on their way to and from the United States. Tourists from France and other European countries stay longer but not always in hotels. Most of them come to visit relatives or friends who are expatriate workers in Tahiti.

Tourism in French Polynesia is still less developed than in Hawaii. High prices and the perceived distance from the United States, Europe, and Asia

When President Harry Truman declared US sovereignty over the natural resources of an adjacent continental shelf in 1945, other countries followed suit, and in 1958 the United Nations convened the Conference on the Law of the Sea, which accepted national control over shelves up to 600 feet (183 m) deep. However, national claims multiplied so much that a second conference was convened, leading to the signing of the Law of the Sea in Jamaica in 1982.

The Law of the Sea states that a country can claim twelve nautical miles of sea off its shores as its territorial waters. (One international nautical mile is equal to around 1.15 miles or 1.85 km.) A country's continental shelf extends two hundred nautical miles offshore. This area is called the Exclusive Economic Zone (EEZ), and the state has full control over all resources, living and nonliving, contained in the zone.

French Polynesia can lay claim to more than 3 million square miles (7.8 million square km) of the continental shelf, with immense possibilities for development. The National Marine Research Center estimates that vast mineral deposits, such as nickel, cobalt, manganese, and copper, are scattered across Tahiti's EEZ. While giving more political weight (and mineral wealth) to oceanic states, the Law of the Sea has also made French Polynesia much more valuable to France. The French government has adamantly refused to give the Territorial Assembly any jurisdiction over Tahiti's EEZ, a clear indication that it does not plan to let go of its sovereignty over the islands.

have kept tourist arrivals low. However, the French Polynesian authorities are targeting to achieve three hundred thousand tourist arrivals per year in the next few years, a figure that is feasible according to experts from the French government. The most popular destinations for tourists are Tahiti, Moorea, Huahine, Raiatea, and Bora Bora.

FISHING

Although industrial fishing has long been dominated by Japanese, Korean, and US purse seiners and long-line vessels, French Polynesia now has a professional fleet trawling its territorial waters. The government has targeted the fishing industry as a major source of future revenues, so it has

A fisherman poses with a dogtooth tuna he caught in Tahitian waters.

invested heavily in storage and packaging facilities as well. Much emphasis is placed on the training of fishermen (only men work on the fishing vessels) so that the industry is run in a more efficient and safe way. The catch is made up of deep-sea fish, mainly tuna, which is highly prized by the Japanese, as well as marlin and shark. Some 8,000 to 10,000 tons (7257 to 9072 metric tons) of fish are caught commercially in French Polynesia each year.

Most Tahitians fishing in the open sea still do so in *bonitiers* (boh-nee-TIAY), 36-foot (11-m) boats propelled by a powerful motor. A *bonitier* can take two or three fishers out for one day to about 30 miles (48 km) from shore. Fishing is done with lines, and the shoals of fish are detected by the presence of birds hovering above the sea. In addition, several sunken barges placed near the coast attract big fish and make it easier to locate large concentrations of fish.

Lagoon fishing is much more common throughout the islands. It is practiced in small wooden boats powered by outboard motors. Swift and light, they are ideal for catching flying fish or mahimahi (also known as dorado or dolphin fish) that are harpooned as they swim by. Lagoon fishers are not professionals; most of them fish for their family meal. When they catch more fish than required, they keep it for the next day's meal.

LE TRUCK

Public transportation in Tahiti is provided by a network of privately owned minibuses called *le truck* (luh TRUCK). The driver's cabin is separated from the passengers' section by a panel, and the passenger door is at the back. Passengers sit on long wooden benches, and bags and other bulky items are piled on the roof of the vehicle. A notice advises passengers to hang their fish from the back of the minibus. The vehicles are painted in bright colors, and the network covers the whole island. The central terminal is near Papeete market, and the last trucks leave for the outlying districts at about 5 p.m. Around town, the service does not stop until 10 or 11 p.m. On Sundays, however, le truck does not run after noon.

The starting point—usually Papeete—and the final destination are indicated at the front of the vehicle. Other district names along the route are painted on the sides. No truck goes around the whole island, and long journeys involve catching several minibuses. In town and also in the districts of Pirae and Faa'a, bus stops are designated by diagonal white lines painted on the street and sometimes with a sign. Elsewhere there is no specific bus stop; passengers just wave down le truck wherever they happen to be. There is no fixed schedule, but the vehicles are more frequent in and around Papeete. Fares are quite cheap and are usually posted on the side.

Inside the minibuses are mammoth speakers that often blast rock music or reggae. At night they take on a different look. Many have softly colored lights inside and play Tahitian ballads instead of loud music.

One of the Le Trucks that transport people around Papeete.

INTERNET LINKS

http://tahiti-tourisme.com.au/about-tahiti/culture/tahitian-black-pearl
This tourism site provides an informative look at Tahiti's black pearl industry.

http://www.tourism-review.com/tourism-in-french-polynesia-now-to-promote-their-culture-news4889
This article details new approaches being tried by Tahiti's tourism industry to bring in more tourists.

ENVIRONMENT

Tropical fish swim and jump in the clean waters of French Polynesia.

5

TRAVEL BROCHURES AND WEBSITES always portray Tahiti as a pristine tropical island. After all, Tahiti depends heavily on its "sun, sand, and sea" tourism, so it wants to show its best self to the world. Naturally, protection of the marine environment is of utmost importance. Most hotels have sewage-treatment facilities and programs for recycling and protection of the beaches. Sustainable development and respect for the environment are regular themes during the annual youth festival organized by the Union pour la Jeunesse de Polynésie (Union of Polynesian Youths). In spite of industrial development, many areas of French Polynesia, even on heavily frequented islands such as Tahiti and Moorea, are indeed in good condition.

The Invasive Species Specialist Group lists the velvet tree, or miconia (*Miconia calvescens*), a native plant of Mexico and South America, as one of the world's one hundred most invasive species. It has caused tremendous ecological destruction in Tahiti, where it is called the "green cancer" because it's rapidly crowding out and killing off the island's native trees. Miconia is similarly wreaking havoc in Hawaii, where it is known as the "purple plague."

But that is not to say the islands don't have environmental problems. The combination of Western lifestyle, modernization, and heavy tourism has created some major concerns. Air and water pollution, waste disposal, destruction of coral reefs, and the decline of certain plant and animal species present particular challenges.

TOURISM

When nearly two hundred thousand people come to visit each year, they create a huge impact on small island environments. The tourists need to eat and drink, thereby requiring an increase in food production. They take showers and flush toilets, impacting fresh water resources; and they make plenty of trash, straining waste management resources. In addition, they use electricity and require transportation, which draws on energy supplies. Not least, tourists need hotels. Tourism, therefore, is the main driving force behind coastal development throughout French Polynesia.

Cruise ships bring tourists to Tahiti.

On the island of Tahiti, inland regions are tough to build in, and in any case, tourists want to be on the ocean. The potential for overcrowding and the increased erosion associated with shoreline development are obvious environmental concerns. Furthermore, climate change is raising ocean levels, which will naturally impact those seaside developments. Although Tahiti rises high above sea level, and could perhaps adapt to changing shorelines, other islands in French Polynesia lie much lower and have more to fear from climate change and the rising sea.

The demand for food—for tourists and residents alike—pushes farmers to use fertilizers and pesticide to increase production. These substances, however, inevitably wash into the ocean, through ground waters or by way of rivers and streams, where they harm the marine environment. Coral reefs in French Polynesia, which support unique and complex ecosystems, are already facing the stress of climate change. The negative effects of coastal development and agricultural runoff are harmful to the extremely vulnerable corals.

FORESTS

About 70 percent of Tahiti is covered with forest, mainly in Tahiti Nui and the mountainous interior of Tahiti Iti. (This is a greater percentage of forest than in French Polynesia as a whole. In that case, 42 percent of the total land is covered in forest.) However, Tahitian forests are not in a healthy state. Apart from encroachments by industrial developments and the human population, the native forest cover has been attacked by imported plant and animal species. Moreover, destructive hurricanes regularly top off the trees or stunt their growth.

A reforestation program has been in place since the late 1970s to replace the trees that are cut down for industrial usage. New seedlings are comprised mainly of the Caribbean pine, but mahogany and teak have also been planted on some islands. Although the program is supervised by the Ministry of Agriculture, the entire process of exploitation and replanting remains in the hands of the private sector.

One danger threatening Polynesian forests is the spread of introduced species such as the velvet tree, or miconia. French Polynesian authorities have experienced some measure of success with the release of a fungus that preys on miconia seedlings. *Colletotrichum gloeosporioides* destroys the leaves of mature velvet trees, causing the trees to die, and also kills the seedlings, especially germinating ones. This two-pronged attack deals with the problem literally at its root, by preventing the miconia seeds from growing into plants, and also by ensuring that mature plants do not reproduce.

In the 1990s the Tahitian sandalwood became endangered because its seeds were being eaten by rats. Following a rescue program, thousands of seeds were collected and planted in controlled areas. The success of the first planting has prompted the Polynesian authorities to enlarge the program to cover more islands.

MARINE ENVIRONMENT

Although 20 percent of the reefs around the urban areas have been destroyed, the coral population in the waters around Tahiti is one of the most stable in the world. In 2005 a team of twenty-eight scientists from nine nations collected a large amount of coral samples that were dissected and studied to reveal changes in sea levels from as far back as twenty-three thousand years ago. Most of the samples came from a location off Maraa, a point separating Tahiti's south and west coasts. The longest sample was 10 feet (3 m) long, representing 350 years of coral growth. Providing a reliable climate record with no gaps, the corals helped the researchers to predict climate variability and piece together the frequency and amplitude of climatic anomalies such as El Niño. Because corals are ultrasensitive to environmental change, they provide a full record of temperature and salinity changes in the South Pacific over their lifetime.

Polynesian waters teem with fish. The most colorful are those living in the coral reefs. They also provide the main source of protein for the island population. Around seven hundred species of fish live in the lagoon or on the reef itself, feeding on the plentiful corals. Among the most attractive are the angelfish, the clown fish, and the damsel fish that live among the pink anemones. The larger parrot fish counts twenty-five varieties in French Polynesia. This brightly colored fish is often eaten raw in salads by the Tahitians. Jacks are also widely represented with seventeen species, and there are a few varieties of mainly harmless lagoon shark. The latter are usually small and can swim in shallow water to look for food.

Fish swim along coral reefs.

Beyond the reef, in the open sea, larger varieties of fish live in deeper waters. Tuna and bonito are the most common. The latter can survive at depths of 900 feet (274 m) and has become a symbol of the Tahitian diet. Barracuda, dorado, and red perch also live in the ocean depths. Six species of marlin can be found in Tahiti, but three have become quite rare: the sailfish, the striped marlin, and the black marlin. The most common is the blue marlin, which can weigh up to a ton. Among the species of deep-sea sharks that frequent Polynesian waters, the gray shark is the most common, followed by the hammerhead shark. The tiger shark stays in deep water during the day and comes out in the channels at night.

Fishing is an important industry in Tahiti, and it is strictly regulated so that the fish stocks have time to renew themselves. Thanks to Tahiti's insistence on sound ecological practices, its marine environment has been quite well preserved. Even the underground nuclear testing on Moruroa and Fangataufa did not affect the level of fish in Polynesian waters. In fact, a recent study has found an unusually large amount of fish around the two atolls.

French Polynesia actively protected whales and other aquatic mammals by setting up a sanctuary in Polynesian waters in 2002. This sanctuary covers the breeding grounds of the twenty-four species of whales that visit French Polynesia regularly, mainly the solitary blue whale, the sperm whale, and especially the humpback, which can be observed by boat between September and November. Rules governing the use of sonar and the distance between a craft and an animal as well as the speed of boats are enforced.

EFFECTS OF NUCLEAR TESTING

French nuclear activity in the Pacific spanned a period of thirty years. France conducted forty-one atmospheric tests between 1966 and 1974, 140 underground tests between 1975 and 1991, and eight more underground tests in 1996. Some of them had a magnitude of 200 kilotons—ten times more powerful than the bomb that leveled the Japanese town of Hiroshima during World War II.

Throughout the testing period, and even to this day, the French authorities have maintained that those tests were clean, with no major repercussions on the local population. Their surveys showed that radiation levels were within limits, and the French defense ministry has always claimed that the data collected from those tests are military secrets.

However, the findings of a committee of inquiry set up by the French Polynesian assembly in 2006 painted a less rosy picture. Based on interviews with former CEP employees, studies of the incidence of cancer in French Polynesia, and twenty-five previously secret defense ministry documents, the committee found that the island of Tahiti itself was subjected to repeated fallout from each of the atmospheric tests more than thirty years ago. Radiation levels on Moruroa and Fangataufa were more than one hundred times above the normal level even during the underground tests.

Figures from the French Cancer Society show six hundred cases of cancer and 250 related deaths a year in French Polynesia out of a total population of 250,000. One study indicated that 25.7 out of every 100,000 French Polynesian women contracted thyroid cancer, compared with 4.8 out of 100,000 in France. Leukemia, which typically manifests itself fifteen to twenty years after radiation exposure, is also on the rise. Moreover, 7.4 percent of former Moruroa workers had physically disabled children, and 2.4 percent had mentally impaired offspring. Experts have also discovered that, even after more than thirty years, some people display chromosomal alterations stemming from irradiation or nuclear contamination.

A group of veterans from Moruroa and Fangataufa set up an association to pressure the French government to come clean on the effects of the tests. The organization Moruroa e Tatou, the Nuclear Worker's Association, sought

ALIEN INVASION

Native to the tropical forests of Central America, the velvet tree (Miconia calvescens) was introduced into Tahiti in 1937 when Harrison W. Smith planted it in his private garden in Papeari. In less than seventy years, the spread of the species has been so rampant that it is now called "the green cancer" by the Tahitians.

Starting out as a shrub, the velvet tree eventually grows into a tree that can reach 50 feet (15 m) in height. Adorned with large velvety leaves, it produces fragrant clusters of pinkish white flowers and sweet purple berries. Because each berry contains between fifty and two hundred seeds and the tree can fruit two or three times a year, the trees have spread at a phenomenal pace.

Miconia calvescens is a threat to the indigenous species of Tahiti because it has become so overwhelmingly dominant that it has taken over about 70 percent of the island's natural forest. Several factors have enabled the tree to proliferate: a lack of natural enemies; the low stature of local trees, which has allowed the velvet tree to tower above them; and a slow reaction by the Tahitian authorities to curb its spread. Moreover, the six hurricanes that hit Tahiti between December 1982 and April 1983 suppressed the growth of the natural forest canopy by breaking the tops of trees and destroying emergent native trees. French Polynesian ecologists estimate that between one-fourth and one-half of all endemic species are now at risk of extinction.

In 1988 the Miconia Research Program was put in place by the Tahitian authorities, and there are now a number of initiatives to slow the growth of the velvet tree.

Māori-style totems form part of the memorial to victims of the French nuclear testing in the Paofai Gardens park in Papeete.

compensation from the French government and helped more than two hundred former workers file class-action suits in the French courts.

In 2008, France finally agreed to pay damages to nuclear test victims, both for veterans and civilians. The process, however, was complex and limited to a small geographical area and certain ailments. About 150,000 veterans and civilians worked on, or were present during, nuclear tests, including 127,000 in Polynesia. But of more than one thousand claims, only nineteen people ever received compensation.

In July 2006, forty years after the first bomb was exploded in Moruroa, the French Polynesian government unveiled a memorial in Papeete to commemorate the 193 tests that had destabilized the region for thirty years. Built in the shape of a traditional *paepae* (PEA-pea), a log seat, with five stones symbolizing the five Polynesian archipelagos, it is not a symbol of reconciliation with France but a sign of reconciliation among Polynesian peoples. In July 2016, the fiftieth anniversary was marked by protest marches, commemorative ceremonies, and educational exhibit in Papeete.

WASTE MANAGEMENT

Tahiti has embarked on an ambitious waste-management program that is unique in the Pacific. Aside from maintaining the infrastructure, the program provides the local population with in-depth education on recycling and waste disposal. The recycling center of Motu Uta receives more than 3,000 tons (2722 metric tons) of waste a year, mainly glass, paper, drink cans, plastic bottles, and cardboard boxes. These are sorted and compacted before being exported overseas to be recycled in countries such as Singapore, India, and

Australia. However, recycling bins are available mainly on Tahiti and Moorea, and the next step for the Ministry of Environment is to reach out to the outer islands in terms of waste-management education.

Nevertheless, much remains to be done in Tahiti itself, where about 60,000 tons (51,130 t) of non-recyclable waste is produced every year (comparable to mainland France) and unauthorized dumping sites can be found all over the island. Proper treatment of household and industrial waste is carried out at two plants in Tahiti—household and common industrial waste at Pa'ihoro, and industrial and hazardous waste at the new incineration plant in Nivee.

Sewage treatment is carried out mainly in Tahiti, Moorea, and Bora Bora. The larger islands have been aware of the importance of water treatment for some years now, and the situation is quite positive. Although priority is given to those islands with a tourism infrastructure, the aim of the Polynesian authorities is to endow each sizable island with its own treatment plant. One of the themes for public environmental education is not to discard wastes into rivers, as these ultimately make their way to the sea and create an imbalance in the ecosystem.

INTERNET LINKS

http://www.sea.edu/spice_atlas/climate_change_atlas/coral_ecology_and_conservation_in_french_polynesia
Climate change and coral conservation are explored in this article.

http://www.sea.edu/spice_atlas/nuclear_testing_atlas/french_nuclear_testing_in_polynesia
An excellent report about the French nuclear testing and its aftermath is posted on this site.

http://www.worldwildlife.org/ecoregions/oc0113
This page details the condition of forests and forest species in French Polynesia.

TAHITIANS

A young Tahitian man wears a traditional costume for a sunset dance performance on the beach.

6

THE TAHITI OF THREE HUNDRED years ago was populated with one people, who called themselves *Taata Mao'hi*. Westerners came to call them *Polynesians*, after the word *Polynesia,* coined in 1756 by the French writer Charles de Brosses. He applied the term, derived from the Greek for "many islands," to all the Pacific Islands. Today, Tahitians are a mixed people, mostly Polynesian, and still largely defined and ruled by outsiders.

All Tahitians are French citizens. Whatever their ethnic background, they enjoy the same constitutional rights as any other citizens of France.

More than 285,000 people live in French Polynesia, with nearly 65 percent living in Tahiti. Because large areas of Tahiti's interior lands are not habitable, most of the island's residents live in the coastal regions, especially along the northwest coast, in and around Papeete. The urban area of greater Papeete is home to more than 133,600 people. Tahiti and the island of Raiatea are the ethnic melting pots. The population on these islands is composed of Polynesians, Europeans (mainly French), Chinese, and people of mixed descent (Polynesian/European, Polynesian/Chinese, and Chinese/European).

"So what I'm saying is that you who are French, you who are Chinese, and you who are Tahitian—each one of us must possess the same respect for this Polynesian cultural foundation. All of us must look to these beginnings as the source from which to build a new society. Everyone having mutual and equal respect, everyone wanting to preserve the integrity of the culture—that's the starting point.
—Henri Hiro (1944-1990), Tahitian poet and activist, in a 1990 interview, urging a revival of Ma'ohi language and culture in Tahiti

A graph of the population of Tahiti over the past centuries shows a sharp decline in the decades following the discovery of the island by the European explorers. However, since the beginning of the twentieth century, the Tahitian population has been slowly rebuilding itself with lower infant-mortality rates, and longer life expectancies and through immigration. In 2016, life expectancy at birth in Tahiti rose to 77.2 years, compared with 81.8 years in France.

In French Polynesia as a whole, about 78 percent of the population is Polynesian, 12 percent Chinese, and 10 percent European, mostly French. These figures are not broken into mixed ancestries as the census stopped asking for such ethnic information in 1988.

POLYNESIANS

The Polynesians were the first inhabitants of Tahiti. Their ancestors traveled by canoe from Southeast Asia to settle in the scattered islands of the Polynesian Triangle. They call themselves *Taata Mao'hi* (tah-AH-tah mah-OH-hee) or *Taata Tahiti,* meaning "people of Polynesia."

The Polynesian people have the same coloring as their distant ancestors—straight black hair, black eyes, and burnished skin. They have wide-set eyes, a round nose, and full lips. Historically strong, active people, they tend to be well built and graceful. A sedentary modern lifestyle, however, is changing their physical profile, and obesity and its attendant health problems are becoming more pronounced.

Children are greatly cherished and valued in Polynesian society, and families tend to be large with as many as ten children per family. In addition, adoption is a traditional feature of Polynesian society.

Like most other colonized peoples, the *Taata Taata Mao'hi* have lost much of their land to the colonizers and are relegated to the bottom of the economic and social ladder. Most islanders outside of Tahiti are farmers, fishers, or manual workers. The Polynesian culture teaches a sense of sharing and reciprocal generosity, and the pursuit of money and material wealth is still, for the most part, alien. Unemployment is rife among Polynesians. Their economic and cultural situation has resulted in rising dissatisfaction with the French government and growing separatist, nationalistic feelings.

DEMIS

The offspring of early marriages between Polynesians and European colonizers, Demis (deh-MEE) are also called *Afa* (AH-fah) *Tahiti*, meaning "half Polynesian." The Demi population displays the whole spectrum of skin colors typical of their ancestors, with many looking no different from Polynesians.

Six Tahitian women pose in front of a painted background in this 1880 photo. Four wear traditional clothing and two wear Western dresses.

When the term *Demi* first appeared, it was used to designate those who started out as traders and landowners. Today, while there are many poor farmers among the Demis, this group is on the whole wealthier than the Polynesians. Indeed, *Demi* has come to signify those Polynesians or mixed-ancestry Polynesians who occupy high-status or powerful social positions or maintain a "European" lifestyle. Fluent in both French and Tahitian, the Demi population acts as a link between the French administration and the local people, although they identify more with European culture.

Contemporary Demis are now teachers, civil servants, and professionals. The largest business firms in the country are in the hands of a few Demi families. Generally speaking, these wealthy Demis do not identify at all with the Polynesians, although they have Polynesian relatives.

Historically, prominent Demi families owned large tracts of land in Tahiti. When their European ancestors arrived in Tahiti, they married the daughters of the tribal chiefs. The land, which used to be owned collectively by the tribe, became the property of the chiefs at the time of colonization and was passed on from them to their mixed descendants. This was how the Salmon family, who come from the line of Queen Marau, the last queen of Tahiti, became one of the most prominent families in the country.

MAUI, THE POLYNESIAN SUPERHERO

In ancient legends, Maui was a Demigod who reveled in playing tricks and upsetting the status quo. One of his best-known exploits was slowing the passage of the sun. Before this feat, the sun used to race across the sky, and days were not long enough for people to beat out and dry tree bark for cloth, to grow and prepare food, and to build temples to the gods.

To slow the sun, Maui braided several lassos, which he threw around the rays of the sun. They all broke, except the one made from the hair of his sister Hina. From then on, the sun was bound to a boulder on the beach and traveled at a more convenient pace. As proof of this exploit, Tahitians point to his footprints, which, legend has it, can still be seen on the reef at Vairao on the peninsula.

Other feats performed by this superhero were lifting the sky high enough to permit people to walk upright, stealing fire from the gods and giving it to humans (making him the Polynesian equivalent of the mythical Greek hero Prometheus), and fishing all the islands of Polynesia out of the sea with a magical hook made from the jawbone of his grandmother. Maui was the archetypal hero who could deal with both gods and humans.

CHINESE

The first Chinese people came to Tahiti during the American Civil War, when the supply of cotton to Europe was disrupted. In 1865 and 1866, a British colonizer recruited 1,010 laborers from the southern Chinese province of Guangdong to work in the cotton fields of Atimaono because the local Polynesians could not be persuaded to do such heavy work. However, at the end of the war, the Tahitian cotton industry went bankrupt, and most of these workers returned to China.

About three hundred Chinese stayed on in Tahiti, taking gardening jobs or becoming shopkeepers. They were joined in 1910 by a group of immigrants fleeing the poverty of their native land. Chinese immigration did not end until World War II. As the government did little to integrate the *Tinito* (tee-NEE-toh), or Chinese, community into Tahitian society, refusing to grant them the right to own land and barring them from many professions, the Chinese

Two Chinese
Tahitian men play
a board game.

immigrants turned their energy to the retail trade. Within a few decades they were in control of the retail trade and of transactions involving vanilla, as well as mother-of-pearl, and were making large capital investments in maritime transportation as well.

In 1964, the French government decided to assimilate the Chinese community by granting them citizenship, requiring that they adopt French names, and closing all Chinese schools. Despite becoming French citizens, the Chinese community is still distinct through the maintenance of language and ancestral customs by way of cultural associations and clan groups. The Chinese shopkeeper is a common sight in all the islands of French Polynesia, and entire streets in Papeete are lined with Chinese stores.

POPA'A

White people are called *Popa'a* (poh-pah-AH), meaning "foreigner," by the Tahitians. The French are also called *Popa'a Farani* (poh-pah-AH fah-rah-NEE). There is no traditional white community in Tahiti, because the former colonizers married Polynesian women, and their descendants are Demis rather than Popa'a. Most Popa'a are French soldiers and civil servants and are only temporary residents in Tahiti. After the closure of the CEP, the French population decreased by half, and now make up only about 4 percent of the total. There had been considerable European immigration in the 1960s and 1970s associated with the setting up of the CEP.

Now that the military presence in Tahiti is greatly reduced due to the closure of the CEP, there is a better statistical balance between the sexes among the Popa'a, with only slightly more males than females. On the whole, the Popa'a community is young and open to change.

Many Popa'a come to Tahiti, live and work in the country, but leave without ever truly assimilating into Polynesian society. Because of the high salaries and other perks offered to French civil servants and administrators, a tour of duty in Tahiti is highly desirable and is treated like a long vacation.

TAHITIAN DRESS

The image that many people associate with Tahiti is that of the bare-breasted *vahine* (vah-HEE-nay), or woman, dressed in a grass skirt with a garland of flowers around her neck. But she can be found only on tourist brochures. The traditional dress for both men and women is the *pareu*, a 6-foot (1.8-m) length of cotton cloth printed with bright designs, usually flowers. There are several ways for women to wear a pareu. The simplest is to wrap the cloth around the body and tuck the ends in. For a more secure fit, the pareu is wrapped around the body, with one corner thrown over the right shoulder, the other corner passed under the left arm, and the two ends tied at the neck. Men wear the pareu as a loincloth, tied around the waist.

When the missionaries arrived in Tahiti, they were shocked by the state of undress of the women in particular and designed a "mission dress" for them. This is a loose cotton dress with wrist- or elbow-length sleeves, much like a nightgown. Cool and comfortable, it is still worn by Tahitian women and is the uniform of *himene* (hee-MAY-nay), or singing, groups.

Most Tahitians, however, dress in stylish Western clothes. Young girls wear jeans and T-shirts or skirts and blouses. At the beach or for casual wear, shorts and cropped tops are common. Tahitian men wear shirts and trousers to work and are often dressed in shorts and T-shirts at home. Men and women put on shoes to go out, although it is customary to remove their shoes in the house.

Three Tahitian men wear traditional pareus, or sarongs, in this photo from 1880.

INTERNET LINKS

http://www.everyculture.com/Cr-Ga/French-Polynesia.html
This site has information about the people of French Polynesia.

https://www.lakeforest.edu/academics/programs/environmental/courses/es368/harris.php
A report on Tahitian cultural identity and activism is posted on this educational site.

LIFESTYLE

Open air huts are a typical example of traditional Tahitian architecture.

7

WHEN THE FRENCH ARTIST PAUL Gauguin first arrived in Papeete in 1891, he was seeking an exotic tropical idyll. Instead, he was disappointed to find a very Westernized society much like the one he had left back in France, but with a better climate. To his horror, the island even had electricity!

Today, of course, after more than 175 years of French rule, Tahiti remains quite Westernized, and Tahitians live a modern lifestyle, particularly in the urban regions. Most of the population of Tahiti is concentrated in and around Papeete. Residents work in the airport, at the docks, and in businesses in town. The rural Tahitians are farmers and fishers, mostly at subsistence level.

Great differences in income have created several distinct social classes, and because the cost of living is very high, many Tahitians live on the brink of poverty. In addition, high unemployment among the young has resulted in severe social problems such as drug addiction, alcoholism, and crime.

However, in spite of difficult living conditions, the Tahitian people have not lost their ability to enjoy themselves. They take pleasure in simple activities, such as listening to music or riding around the island on their scooters.

Hotels and resorts in Tahiti often make use of native architectural styles in their construction, including rounded forms, large openings for ventilation, natural materials, and plant life to create a sense of authentic experience. However, the bungalows and huts also incorporate modern luxuries to cater to tourists' expectations.

CLASS STRUCTURE

The Tahitian social structure is very much related to the ethnic backgrounds of the people. The Popa'a are at the top of the social ladder, followed by the Demis and the Chinese, with the Polynesians at the bottom. Even so, class stratification is based not so much on heritage as on affluence.

UPPER CLASS The upper class is formed by the French civil servants and administrators, who are paid salaries that are almost double those of their counterparts in France. However, while they receive generous expatriation benefits, they also incur high expenses if they want to consume French products, since these tend to be very expensive. Most Popa'a government officials serve a three- or four-year term in the territory, at the end of which they are entitled to six months' paid leave. Although they try to get into the spirit of life in Polynesia, by wearing flowery shirts to work, for example, the ruling class lives apart from the local population. The French officials' exalted status attracts much resentment from the local population, who would like to see fewer of them and more of their own people in charge of their country.

MIDDLE CLASS The middle class is made up of Demis—people of mixed ancestry. Although some Demis are far more affluent than the Popa'a, they are not considered to be on an equal footing with the French community. Many Demis families are wealthy landowners who derive their income from leasing the land to farmers or developing their property into commercial ventures. Because they have always had access to formal education, the Demis often hold jobs in the government service and in professional occupations and still keep a strong hold on the business sector. They are generally fluent in French, and many can also speak English. Culturally closer to their European roots, they are faced with a situation where the two sides of their ancestry are at odds with each other. Economically powerful, they do not have any political clout. However, most Demis are against independence and side with the French population on political matters.

In terms of income, the Chinese community also belongs to the middle class. Having succeeded in the retail trade, the Chinese have moved into

bigger businesses and bought up large areas of property since being granted French citizenship. Today most Chinese manage their own businesses, and many of the young people, having received a formal French education, are professionals. They are not formally represented in the government as a group, but some politicians are of mixed Chinese ancestry. The Chinese have economic power, but they have no cultural ties with the traditional Demi middle class. Having long been viewed as an economic threat to the local upper class, this community has been slowly assimilating into Tahitian society through marriage with Polynesians and Popa'a, forming a new, ethnically different Demi group. The Chinese community is politically fragmented, with one group favoring independence and the other preferring the status quo that has allowed them to amass their wealth.

LOWER CLASS The lower class is formed primarily of the majority Polynesian ethnic group. Despoiled of their land during colonization, most rural Polynesians subsist on farms rented from the wealthy landowners.

Middle class homes sit on a hillside road in a Papeete neighborhood.

Those who own land are vegetable farmers, supplementing their diet with fish that they catch themselves. Most other Polynesians are employed as manual workers, in the construction industry, or in tourism. Unemployment among Polynesians is very high. The outskirts of the capital are surrounded by slums where crime and prostitution are rife. In the shantytowns behind Papeete and Faa'a, there are typically ten to fifteen Polynesians living crammed into each neat flower-decked plywood house. Polynesian families tend to be larger than those of other ethnic groups. Disaffected Polynesian youths were responsible for much of the looting and violence committed during the antinuclear protests of September 1995. The poor urban communities view independence from France as their only means of salvation.

A small group of poor Demis is also part of the lower class. Because of their poverty, they feel closer to the Polynesian section of the population. For all intents and purposes, these Demis are treated as Polynesians.

THE TAHITIAN HOUSE

The traditional Tahitian residence consists of several separate buildings instead of rooms. The *fare tutu* (fah-RAY too-TOO) is the kitchen, while the dining area is the *fare tamaa* (fah-RAY tah-MAH-ah). The sleeping quarters are located in another building called the *fare taoto* (fah-RAY tah-OH-toh). In addition, toilet and bathing facilities are located in separate buildings. The traditional building materials are coconut trunks and pandanus leaves.

Today very few Tahitians live in traditional houses. Traditional design has been replaced by Western architectural models. In the rural areas, houses are square, built of wood, and covered with a sloping thatch roof. In the affluent suburbs of Papeete, people live in Western-style detached houses made of concrete and fronted by flower-filled gardens. Most working-class Tahitians, however, live in double-story row houses made of plywood. These are small, afford almost no privacy, and have no garden. Although such houses are ugly and uncomfortable, public housing is still better than the slums, where several families share a house and as many as twenty people live in one room.

HEALTH CARE

Health care in Tahiti is of the same standard as that in France, with doctors in Papeete's Mamao Hospital treating almost every type of disease and the former military hospital of Jean Prince in Pirae specializing in cardiology. The hospitals in the other towns all possess an operating room, but severe cases are sent to Papeete.

Tahitians generally have three health-care options: traditional remedies, private doctors, and public health services. *Raau* (rah-AH-oo) *Tahiti*, or traditional medicine, is composed of herbal remedies prepared at home, which are quite effective in the treatment of pains and aches, coughs, and fever. Traditional remedies are still very popular for cultural reasons and also because they are cheap. The traditional medicine man is called a *tahua* (tah-HOO-ah) and gives treatments for free. Most people do not actually consult a *tahua*, because the recipes for common remedies are passed down in the family from one generation to the next.

Private medical facilities are good but more costly in comparison with public health services. They include general practitioners, specialists, and dentists. Two modern clinics—Paofai and Cardella—in Papeete offer surgical and maternity facilities. They also employ a number of doctors who give consultations to the sick. Public health care is free and available at dispensaries, polyclinics, and hospitals. Schoolchildren receive regular free health screenings.

The Ta'aone Hospital in Papeete is one of the modern health care centers in Tahiti.

EDUCATION

Tahitian children follow the French system of education. Schooling is compulsory between the ages of five and sixteen. After secondary school, the better students study three more years for the baccalaureate exams. Those who pass receive nearly free university education.

The French Polynesian government is in charge of primary and secondary education, while tertiary education is still the domain of the French government. Tahitian children study a hybrid curriculum, learning both French and Tahitian language and literature and the history and geography of both France and their own part of the world. The best students are given scholarships by the government to further their studies. Those who prefer can move on to vocational training in a Centre de Jeunes Adolescents (CJA), or Center for Young Adolescents. They start at the age of thirteen and stay for four years.

There are two types of schools: government schools, which are free, and private schools, usually run by the churches. Most primary schools are public, but more than half of the young people of Papeete attend a private secondary school. Many of the private schools receive government funding. In exchange for this, they must follow the same curriculum as government schools.

Higher education is provided by the Université de la Polynésie Française (University of French Polynesia), founded in 1999 in Puna'auia. It has about more than three thousand students, including students pursuing advanced degrees, and more than one hundred professors and teachers.

SOCIAL PROBLEMS

One of the main problems faced by Tahitian society today is unemployment. The unemployed consist mainly of women, young people, people with few skills, and Polynesians. More than half of the people looking for work are in the eighteen to twenty-four age group. In addition to the unemployed, there are wage earners who are employed on a periodic basis. Frequently out of work but not registered as unemployed, they account for as much as 30 percent of the labor force.

ALCOHOLISM AND DRUG ABUSE

One of the scourges of Tahiti, alcoholism is a source of major social dysfunction in Tahitian society, particularly among Polynesians and other lower-income groups. Drinking beer is almost a rite of passage for young boys, who see it as taking a step into the adult world. The legal drinking age is twenty-one, but the usual age at which boys start drinking alcohol is around fourteen. Drinking is very common among the lower class, and alcoholism and its negative effects are seen as unavoidable. Indeed, Tahitians are often impressed by good drinkers, and the ability to consume large amounts of alcohol can even be a source of pride. Excessive drinking is a problem that also affects women and girls. Domestic violence is the most frequent consequence of excessive consumption of alcohol. Another consequence is road accidents caused by drunk driving.

Drug addiction is not as prevalent as drunkenness but is cause for concern, with children as young as ten years old having been caught abusing solvents. Hard drugs, such as heroin and cocaine, are still relatively uncommon in Tahiti, but the cultivation of marijuana by small-scale traffickers is spreading in the humid, mountainous regions of the interior.

Young Polynesians who have dropped out of school at sixteen—the age when compulsory education ends—and are waiting to enlist in the military are particularly vulnerable. With a lot of time on their hands and little money, and tempted by Papeete's consumer society, some turn to petty crime such as theft. Young people from low-income families tend to live in groups and call themselves *hombos* (HOM-boh). The word derives from the Spanish *hombre* (man) and is used to describe "antiheroes" such as Mexican and US outlaws and comic-book characters.

Many sociologists believe that these young Polynesians turn to petty crime because they are confused about their own cultural identity, living in a world with two different, often conflicting, cultures—Polynesian and French.

VAHINE

Two centuries ago, the French explorer Bougainville wrote that Tahitian *vahine* (vah-HEE-nay), or women, were as pretty as European women and better proportioned. Since then, the myth of the gentle women of Tahiti,

THE THIRD SEX

Before the arrival of the Europeans and their strict attitudes regarding sexuality, the indigenous cultures of the Pacific Islands took a far more permissive view of such matters. In particular, Tahitian society was very accepting of variations within gender identity. The mahu *was—and still is—a person of uncertain or mixed gender, sometimes called "the third sex." Typically, this a person with a male body who displays female attributes and may wear women's clothing.*

Polynesia's mahus *(mah-HOO) suffer little of the stigma attached to transvestites in the West. When the missionaries first arrived in Tahiti, they were shocked to discover that not only did the* mahus *exist but also that they were encouraged to take on the jobs women normally did. They looked after children, worked as maids, and cooked, all the while wearing women's clothes or whatever else they wanted to wear. In festival performances and celebrations, they sometimes assumed the roles played by women. European missionaries and authorities naturally outlawed and demonized such behavior, but it never disappeared. Indeed, the French artist Paul Gauguin, who famously lived in Tahiti in the late nineteenth century, associated with mahus and a number of gender-ambiguous people appear in his paintings.*

In the past, a young boy's parents might choose the "man-woman" role for him, but today it is only by his own choice. Mahus perform domestic tasks designated for women and may eventually find jobs usually performed by women, such as waiting on tables in a restaurant, cleaning rooms in a hotel, or working as a bartender. Usually only one mahu *exists in each village or community, evidence that the* mahu *serves a certain sociological function in Tahitian society.*

Though Tahitians may poke fun at mahus, *they are fully accepted in society, with some even teaching Sunday school. However, the influx of Western attitudes has also brought some disparagement to a gender that was once fully acknowledged. Some, but not all,* mahus *are homosexual. Mahus even have special beauty contests, such as Miss Raerae or Miss Tane (tane is Tahitian for "man").*

half-naked and beckoning to all new male arrivals, has taken root in Western imagination. The romanticized vahine has long black hair, a slim and supple body, and a bewitching smile.

Most Tahitian women of all ages like to wear colorful hibiscus or frangipani blooms in their hair and clothes of bright, vivid colors. Even the simplest housedress is worn with style. Tahitian women wear very little jewelry, preferring the flowers that grow in profusion on their island. The art of making flower garlands and headdresses is passed down from mother to daughter. The flowers are picked before sunrise, and it takes about a half-hour to make one simple headdress.

In the days when the first European explorers marveled at their apparent freedom, Tahitian women were in fact treated as second-class citizens. Most families did not value their daughters as highly as their sons. Women were expected to be obedient and submissive.

Today's vahine enjoy more equality with men. Tahitian women are given the same educational opportunities and they work as teachers, scientists, and truck drivers.

INTERNET LINKS

http://www.sea.edu/spice_atlas/tahiti_atlas/urbanization_in_ tahiti_papeetes_domino_effect
This excellent report looks at urban culture in Papeete.

http://www.tate.org.uk/context-comment/articles/men-women-pacific
This interesting article about the mahu of Tahiti was written to accompany a Paul Gauguin exhibit in 2010.

http://www.thetahititraveler.com/general-information/histoire/ how-did-polynesian-live
This travel site describes how Polynesians lived before Westernization.

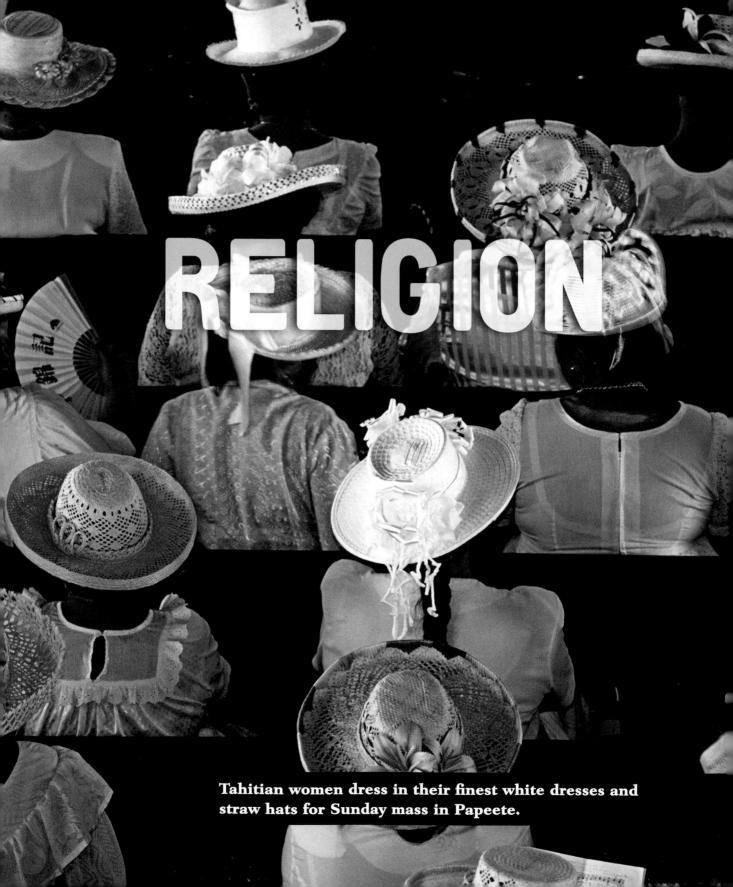

RELIGION

Tahitian women dress in their finest white dresses and straw hats for Sunday mass in Papeete.

8

TAHITIANS ARE VERY DEVOUT, despite decades of secular living. Church attendance is very high, and many children attend schools run by the churches. Although Tahiti is administered by France, a country where the main religion is Roman Catholicism, the majority of Tahitians are Protestants of the Evangelical Church. This is because the first Europeans to settle on the island were Protestant missionaries from the London Missionary Society. After an unsuccessful early attempt, Catholic missionaries returned thirty-nine years after the Protestant missionaries, and the Mormons followed eight years later.

Today, in addition to the Evangelical, Catholic, and Mormon churches, Seventh-Day Adventists, Jehovah's Witnesses, and Sanitos are represented in Tahiti. A few among the Chinese populace are Buddhists.

Although the government recognizes no official religion, government meetings often begin with a few prayers.

In Tahiti, most Sunday services are well attended. In some congregations, parishioners dress in solid white, with women wearing a white mission dress and a white hat, and men wearing a white shirt and slacks. Services are conducted in Tahitian and last up to two hours. The whole congregation joins the choir in singing beautiful hymns or songs of worship and praise.

Prior to the introduction of Christianity at the end of the eighteenth century, Tahitians had their own ancient religion. They believed in the immortality of the soul, in a heavenly paradise, and in reincarnation as another creature "on land, in the sea, or in the skies." When King Pomare II became a Christian, many sacred statues and other religious symbols were destroyed. The conversion to Christianity was total, and there are no followers of the ancient religion today.

However, in both Protestant and Catholic churches, Ma'ohi cultural identity plays a strong role in the theology and customs. Elements of the old religion, such as a focus on the sacred earth and ancestral traditions, are merged with the Christian teachings. Modern native Polynesians are reviving the old cultures and beliefs in an effort to reclaim their heritage.

THE EVANGELICAL CHURCH

More than half of the population of Tahiti is Protestant. The first missionaries from the London Missionary Society arrived in 1797. Made up of Presbyterians, Methodists, and Episcopalians, the mission did not meet with success until 1812, when King Pomare II converted to the new faith for strategic reasons. Thereafter all Tahitians became Christians, and the Pomare rulers staunchly upheld their faith. So influential were the Evangelical missionaries that one of them, George Pritchard, tried to convince Queen Pomare IV to petition the English king to make Tahiti a British protectorate. This started a conflict with the French that led to the eventual annexation of Tahiti by France.

The Tahitian population was initially very hostile to Christianity, yet there were some similarities between their traditional religion and the Christian faith—Ma'ohi legends that resemble Biblical stories; the existence of a deity, Ta'aroa, creator of the universe; and the belief in an immortal soul. After the initial wariness and reticence of Tahitians wore off, these similarities must have facilitated the implantation of Christianity in Tahiti. Also, Polynesian belief systems allowed for the possibility of adopting new and more powerful gods, such as those followed by conquering chiefs. Thus, the technological superiority displayed by the Europeans could have been interpreted as a sign of a more powerful god who was worthy of adoption.

Formerly known as the Evangelical Church of French Polynesia, the organization changed its name in 2004 to the Ma'ohi Protestant Church. The church is organized into ninety-six congregations, each led by a pastor and a council of deacons. The most important Protestant church in Tahiti is the Temple of Pa'ofai in Papeete.

THE CATHOLIC CHURCH

The first attempt at converting the Tahitians to Catholicism took place in 1774, when two Franciscan priests were left on the island to spread the faith. They were so fainthearted that the mission failed dismally. Mistaking the curiosity of the natives for aggression, the priests locked themselves up in the mission building and concluded that Tahiti was too dangerous for them. They went back to Peru one year later, leaving no trace of their passage.

The next Catholic missionaries arrived from France in 1834 but were sent away by Queen Pomare IV upon the advice of the British missionary and consul George Pritchard. It was not until the French established the protectorate that the Catholic Church gained more influence.

Today half of the people in northern Tahiti are Catholic—mainly the Popa'a government workers. They are concentrated in the urban region between Paea and Mahina, where most French expatriates live. Overall 30 percent of the population of French Polynesia is Catholic.

The Catholic Church is very influential in the field of social services. It runs seventeen primary schools and secondary schools in Tahiti. One of the largest is La Mennais, a Catholic middle and high school in Papeete with more than two thousand students, and Anne-Marie Javouhey College in Papeete, which has about one thousand students. The church is also active in the formation and running of youth organizations, including the Boy Scouts and the Sporting and Cultural Federation of France. In addition, the church conducts family-planning classes, organizes counseling sessions for families, and prepares young people for married life. The use of the media is vital for

THE LONGEST TEMPLE IN THE WORLD

After King Pomare II became a Christian, he decided to emulate the biblical King Solomon and build a temple larger than that of Jerusalem.

Knowing nothing about Hebrew or European architecture, he based his temple on a traditional oval hut, using native timber and palm leaves. This method of construction enabled the temple to be built in less than a year. The central roof ridge rested on thirty-six pillars made of full-length breadfruit trees, and the lower edges of the roof rested on 280 shorter pillars of the same material. The walls, straight on the long sides but circular at the short ends, were made of sawed planks. The roof was covered with pandanus leaves.

Called the Royal Mission Chapel, the temple was 712 feet (217 m) long. However, due to the insufficiency of building materials and construction techniques, the width was only 54 feet (16.5 m) and the height 18 feet (5.5 m). By comparison, Saint Peter's Basilica in Rome is 616 feet (188 m) long, 379 feet (115.5 m) wide, and 151 feet (46 m) high (without the cupola). The Royal Mission Chapel had 29 doors and 133 windows with sliding shutters to let in air and light. Because of its strange proportions, it looked more like a huge, flattened cowshed than the awe-inspiring monument that its builder intended it to be.

The corridor-shaped building could accommodate a congregation of six thousand people, as happened once or twice a year during the general church assemblies. However, no preacher could make himself heard by everyone. This problem was eventually solved by the erection of three pulpits: the first in the eastern nave, where the king sat with his nobles on wooden benches; the second in the middle; and the third in the western nave, where the commoners sat on a layer of dry grass spread out on the floor. The separation of the social classes was facilitated by a natural obstacle: a river 5 feet (1.5 m) wide, which the builders had not been able to divert, flowing diagonally across the floor.

With the death of Pomare II in 1821, the Royal Mission Chapel began to decay. It was eventually replaced by a wooden church of more manageable size, which was torn down at the end of the nineteenth century to make way for a charming twelve-sided chapel. This was replaced by a slightly larger one in 1978.

the church to reach as many Tahitians as possible. Two Catholic newspapers are published, a bimonthly in French and a monthly in Tahitian. The Tepano Jaussen Center also prepares radio and television programs.

Most Catholic churches in Tahiti are found in the urban sprawl of Papeete. The oldest and most important is Notre Dame Cathedral, built in 1875. Many new church buildings reflect modern architectural trends. The Saint Etienne Church in Puna'auia has an interesting facade of overlapping triangles. Services are usually conducted in French and are characterized by immense fervor and beautiful singing.

OTHER CHURCHES

Five smaller churches are active in Tahiti: the Church of Jesus Christ of Latter-day Saints (Mormons), Seventh-Day Adventists, Jehovah's Witnesses, the Reorganized Church of Jesus Christ of Latter-day Saints (Sanitos), and the Pentecostal Movement. Young Mormon missionaries continue to flock to Tahiti from the United States for two-year stays. They travel in pairs and are easily recognizable by their attire: short-sleeve white shirts with a tie. All five churches are characterized by the payment of tithes and their rejection of the established churches.

The Mormons, the Sanitos, and the Seventh-Day Adventists run their own schools and organize activities for young people and women. Emphasis is placed on the family, and training and personal development are considered important to improve oneself economically.

POLYNESIAN TRADITIONAL BELIEFS

The ancient Polynesian world was inhabited with gods, Demigods, spirits, and elves, all of whom could move freely between this world and theirs. The gods were represented by carved figures called *tikis*. The spiritual power of the gods rested in the *mana*, the essence of divine authority with which high chiefs were also endowed.

The most important place of worship was the *marae* (mah-RAH-ay), a rectangular area covered with paving stones and surrounded by low walls.

There are many Polynesian creation myths, many of which feature the same or similar gods and storylines that overlap or differ slightly.

In one such ancient Tahitian myth, a great octopus held the sky and the earth together in its arms. The god Ta'aroa existed in the darkness of contemplation, and from this darkness he called the other gods into being. (In other accounts, the universe was a great egg (pa'a), and Ta'aroa existed inside its darkness until he cracked its shell with his body.) When Ta'aroa shook himself, feathers fell and turned into trees, plantains, and other green plants.

Ru (the Abyss) killed the octopus with a magic trick, but the octopus still did not release his hold on the universe, and the Demigods Ru, Hina, and Maui were born in the darkness. Ru raised the sky as high as the coral tree but ruptured himself, so

his intestines floated away to become the clouds that usually hang over the island of Bora Bora. Maui, the trickster, then used wedges to support the sky and went to enlist the help of Tane, who lived in the highest heaven.

Tane drilled into the sky with a shell until light came through. The arms of the octopus fell away and became the island of Tubuai. Tane then decorated the sky with stars and set the sun and moon on their courses. The fish and other sea creatures were given places and duties, and the god Tohu was assigned the job of painting the beautiful color on the fishes and the shells of the deep. In Tahiti, Tane is symbolized by a piece of finely braided coconut-fiber rope.

In another myth version, Ta'aroa conjured the first man, Ti'i out of the earth. (Ti'i is sometimes presented as destructive and violent.) Then the god created the first woman, and her name was Hina. She represented good and had the power of birth and rebirth. In Polynesian mythology, Hina is often a cosmological Mother Earth.

The altar, in the form of a step pyramid, stood at one end. Worshippers asked for the gods' blessings by making offerings of fruits, vegetables, fish, pigs, and dogs, which were placed on wooden platforms. Once the gods had sampled each food, the priests carrying out the ceremony consumed the rest.

Human sacrifices were carried out in times of great crisis. Only men could be sacrificed, as women were considered ill-suited vessels for the gods. The victim was ambushed and killed elsewhere before being offered to the gods.

Many restrictions called *tapu* (the origin of the English word "taboo") were observed. Although Tahitians have been Christians for almost two hundred years, there are those who remain wary of going too close to the ancient places of worship.

INTERNET LINKS

http://www.everyculture.com/Oceania/Tahiti-Religion-and-Expressive-Culture.html
Traditional religious belief and customs are addressed on this site.

https://www.oikoumene.org/en/member-churches/maohi-protestant-church
Information about the Mao'hi Protestant Church is found on this World Council of Churches site.

http://www.tahitiguide.com/@en-us/8-5-religion_french_polynesia.htma
http://www.tahitiguide.com/@en-us/8-29-tikis_and_marae.htma
This travel site gives a quick overview of Tahitian religion today, as well as ancient Polynesian beliefs.

http://tahiti-tourisme.com.au/about-tahiti/culture/religions-in-french-polynesia
This tourism site provides a short overview of religious culture in French Polynesia.

LANGUAGE

TU SURFES ici DEMAIN?

NETTOIE UN PEU AUJOURD'HUI

In French, the sign reads, "Are you surfing here tomorrow? Clean up a little today."

TAHITI HAS TWO OFFICIAL languages: Tahitian and French. Official documents and speeches are generally in French and are rarely translated. Most people are fluent in French, although some Polynesians, particularly those from the lower strata of Tahitian society, speak only Tahitian. Many of the expatriate civil servants, on the other hand, do not understand Tahitian.

English is taught as a third language in some secondary schools, and many educated Demis and Chinese can speak it quite well. Most people employed in the tourist industry can manage a simple conversation in English. Large Chinese stores also have someone who can speak English, although most Chinese use Hakka, a Chinese dialect, among themselves.

THE TAHITIAN LANGUAGE

Tahitian is one of a family of Austronesian languages spoken from Madagascar in the Indian Ocean through Indonesia all the way to Easter Island and Hawaii. Among Polynesian languages, those of Eastern Polynesia and New Zealand (Tahitian, Hawaiian, Māori) are quite different from those of Western Polynesia (Samoan, Tongan). Within French Polynesia, the Tahitian language is spoken mainly in the Society Islands. However, with the improvement of interisland communications

Traditionally, the Tahitian language had no written form. History, customs, and traditions were passed down from one generation to the next by word of mouth. In 1797, the British Protestant missionary Henry Nott arrived in Tahiti and learned the language. He worked with King Pomare II to invent a written form and then translated the Bible into the Tahitian language.

This sign says "Private Parking" in both French and Tahitian.

and the growing dominance of Tahiti over the rest of the territory, the dialects in the outer islands are increasingly influenced by Tahitian.

There are eight consonants in Tahitian (*f, h, m, n, p, r, t, v*) and five vowels (*a, e, i, o, u*). Vowels can be either long or short. The small number of letters means that many words are spelled the same way; the difference is indicated by how long the vowel is held when pronounced. One interesting feature of Tahitian words is the inclusion of two or three consecutive vowels, sometimes the same vowel (as in *Faa'a*). Each vowel is pronounced separately, except for *ai, au, ae,* and *oi,* which are usually pronounced as diphthongs. There are no appearances of two consecutive consonants. An important sound in the Tahitian language is the glottal stop, which usually separates two vowel sounds. The glottal stop is produced by raising the back of the mouth to block the flow of air before pronouncing the next vowel, as in the English "uh-oh." Two words spelled the same way can be differentiated by the use of the glottal stop. In written texts, it is sometimes represented by a ', a straight apostrophe.

A sentence is made up of the verb, the subject, and the object, in this order. Nouns do not have singular and plural forms, nor do they have gender. To denote the plural, the word *mau* (mah-OO) is added before the noun. To denote the masculine, the word *tane* (tah-NAY), or "man," follows the noun, while the word *vahine,* or "woman," following the noun means that it is a feminine word.

Just like any other living language, Tahitian is constantly changing. The influence of English is evident in the following words: *faraipani* (frying pan), *moni* (money), *painapo* (pineapple), and *tapitana* (captain). These influences, however, are not recent but date back to initial contact with English missionaries in particular.

TAHITIAN PRONUNCIATION

Consonants

f	*as in* four
h	*as in* home, *except when it is preceded by* i *and followed by* o *or* u; *then it sounds like* sh
m	*as in* man
n	*as in* nine
p	*as in* super, *while blowing as little air as possible*
r	*a rolled sound produced by caving in the tip of the tongue, similar to the French pronunciation*
t	*as in* paste, *with no explosion of air*
v	*as in* vain, *but sometimes also pronounced like a* w *or almost like a* b *with both lips touching*

In some words, r *and* n *are used interchangeably;* f *and* h *are also used as variants of each other.*

Vowels

a	*as in* ah
e	*as in* pay
i	*as in* till
o	*as in* hose
u	*as in* good

Long vowels are read the same as listed above but pronounced as if they were doubled.

FRENCH

In Tahiti, the use of French depends greatly on the speaker's level of education. Demi families, having had access to education for several generations, are very fluent in both languages. They use French at home and on social occasions. Tahitian is spoken by "Polynesian" families (regardless of ethnicity), who have maintained the language in spite of restrictions on its

A flower-bedecked woman reads a newspaper in a Tahitian market.

usage in the school systems prior to the 1980s. However, proper French is less widely used by poor Demi families in rural areas, where access to education may be limited.

French is the working language in Papeete. In general, all official matters are conducted in it and school is taught in French. The Tahitians speak French with a flourish, giving it a special richness with their rolled *r*'s.

MEDIA AND COMMUNICATIONS

Tahiti is a fully developed country, and enjoys cell phones, internet, and other communications networks, especially in the urban areas.

NEWSPAPERS The press in Tahiti has a very short history. Officially there was a state-run newspaper in existence called *Messager de Tahiti* (1852—1882). But the first modern newspaper, *Les Nouvelles de Tahiti (The News of Tahiti),* only hit the newsstands in 1957. In 2014, *Les Nouvelles* published its final edition and no longer exists. *La Dépêche de Tahiti (Tahiti Dispatch)*, first published in 1964, remains a daily newspaper with a circulation of about fifteen thousand and maintains a website as well. There is no national newspaper in the Tahitian language.

RADIO, TELEVISION, AND INTERNET Radio operations started in 1935 with a small group of amateur wireless operators broadcasting news and entertainment in the evening. The first radio station, Radio Tahiti—*La Voix de France* ("The Voice of France"), was established in 1949, with programs in French and Tahitian. It has now been absorbed by the French state-controlled Réseau Outre-Mer 1ere (First Overseas Network) which also broadcasts in the other French overseas departments and territories. There are also a small number of privately-owned radio stations. Some are commercial ventures reaching out to specific segments of the population, while others are run by the churches. The most popular is Radio 1, which features local and international news as well as French and international pop music. It also puts on musical concerts for its listeners every year. Tiare FM is 100-percent Polynesian, broadcasting in the Tahitian language and promoting local artists.

Réseau Outre-Mer 1ere also operates two television stations in Tahiti, one in French and the other in Tahitian. Most of the programs are imported from three stations in France and are current affairs programs, variety and game shows, and movies. Tahiti Nui Television, set up with the help of the French Polynesian government in 2004, aims to promote and preserve Polynesian culture through its emphasis on local and regional news, sports, and music. The station offers a mixture of French programs, local news, and documentaries. Canal+, the French private satellite network, is also available in French Polynesia.

In 2015, Internet users in French Polynesia totalled about 183,000, or about 64 percent of the population.

INTERNET LINKS

http://www.omniglot.com/writing/tahitian.htm
Omniglot gives a basic introduction to Tahitian with links to related sites.

http://www.tahiti-infos.com
Tahiti Infos is a French-language news site covering the news of Tahiti, French Polynesia, the Pacific, France, and the world. It provides a Google translation option.

https://www.tripadvisor.com/Travel-g294338-s604/French-Polynesia:Important.Phrases.html
This page offers common phrases in both French and Tahitian along with pronunciation guides.

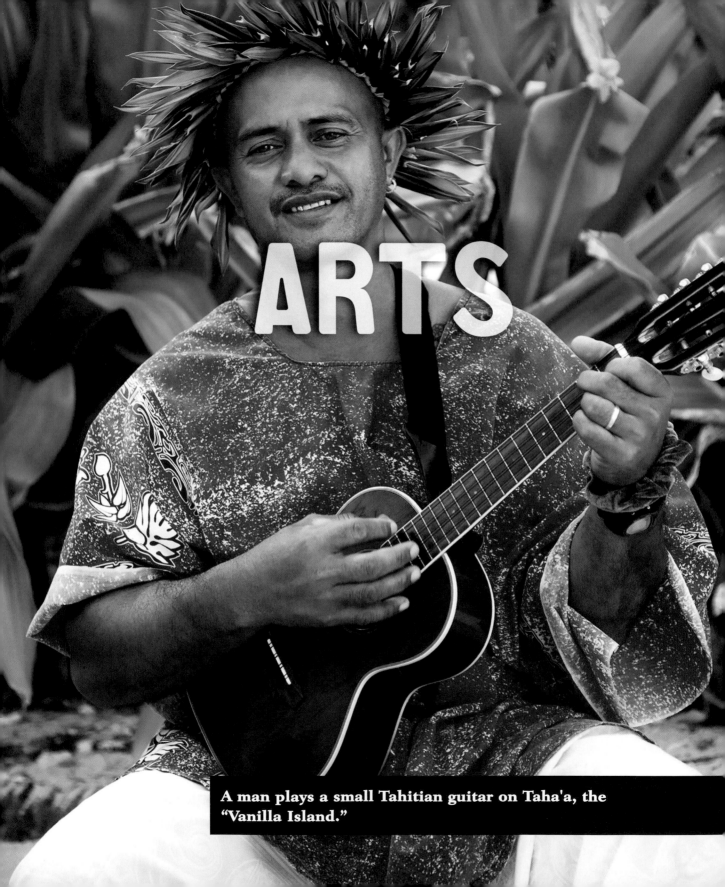

ARTS

A man plays a small Tahitian guitar on Taha'a, the "Vanilla Island."

10

TAHITIANS ARE AN INNATELY artistic people who treasure beauty in their daily lives, as demonstrated by the flower garlands and headdresses they love to weave and wear. Artistry is displayed in every small garden plot, where flowers are grown in harmonious beauty. In the arena of traditional artisan work, however, local Tahitian artists have made their mark. These include quilting and rug and basket weaving (particularly renowned in the Austral Islands), which are done by women. Wood carving by Tahitian artists is much admired in the Marquesas.

Tahitian dancing, banned centuries ago by Europeans who didn't understand or value Polynesian culture, is now the most treasured art form. In fact, Tahitian dance and drumming are inseparable and have become world renowned symbols of Polynesian culture.

"For this renewal (of identity) to continue, Polynesians must write. … They now must write and express themselves. It doesn't matter what language they use, whether it's Mao'hi, French, or English. The important thing is that they write, that they do it! And I think that in a short while we will have Tahitian authors—authors free of insecurities and able to express who we are!"
—Tahitian poet and activist Henri Hiro (1944-1990), in a 1990 interview urging Tahitians to reclaim their land and language through writing.

MUSIC

Music is in the blood of the Tahitian people. At home after work, they sometimes bring out a guitar or a ukulele and sing a few songs as a form of leisure activity. Groups of *fetii* meet on the weekend to and make music. Although they also play traditional Tahitian ballads, they prefer English-language pop songs. Nowadays it is common to bring along a portable stereo to provide the music while everyone sings along, chats, or drinks. No party or outing is complete without music.

Singing in Tahitian is called *himene*, from the English word "hymn." Indeed, the church is where most singing takes place. However, the word also refers to any form of group singing. Himene groups are usually formed on a regional basis, and anyone, young or old, can be a member. Singing is done while seated, with a male soloist leading the group. *Himene tarava* (hee-MAY-nay tah-RAH-vah) consists of a large number of men and women singing a

The traditional Tahitian musical instrument is the drum. Toere (toh-AY-ray) is an unusual drum carved out of one piece of wood. It is basically a hollowed-out tree trunk with a rectangular slit running down the middle. The drummer holds it upright with one end on the floor and beats the side with a stick to produce a staccato beat. Toere come in three sizes, and each size produces a different sound. Some musicians name their toere in order to impart certain spiritual qualities to it or to distinguish it from others.

Fa'atete (fah-AH-tay-tay) is another ancient drum. It is made from a hollowed tree trunk covered with a skin, traditionally shark but today more commonly calf. The

skin is stretched before each performance and loosened afterward. Faatete usually measure 25 inches (61 cm) in height and 12 inches (30 cm) in diameter. Decorative motifs are carved on the sides.

Pahu (pah-HOO) is of Western origin and can be made from wood or cut out from a metal barrel. To produce quality sound, the diameter and the height must be roughly the same: 20–30 inches (51–76 cm). The covering is of calfskin, and the pahu is decorated with paintings. The drum has two skins, but only one side is beaten with a stick. The drummer sometimes uses his hand to hit the other side. The musician is always seated with the pahu on its side in front of him.

cappella (without instrumental accompaniment) in six to ten parts. These complex tunes often narrate ancient Tahitian legends or historical events. *Ute* (OO-tay) is less dignified—a group of men and women sing a refrain in a guttural voice while a soloist improvises a comic or satirical narration.

Himene groups also take part in some dances, such as *aparima* and *hivinau*. On these occasions, they sing to the accompaniment of musical instruments.

DANCING

The Tahitian term for dancing is *ori Tahiti* (oh-REE tah-hih-TIH), which means "Tahitian dancing in the traditional style." Another word commonly used to describe it is *tamure* (tah-MOO-ray).

Tahitian children are exposed to dancing from a young age. Most schools teach dancing as a recreational activity, and local parishes also have their own dance groups where children are introduced to this ancient art form. Whereas the first missionaries viewed Tahitian dancing as obscene and sinful, the churches now promote it as a form of collective activity. Dance groups are formed at various levels, in church or regional groups. Tamure is almost exclusively a group activity. Even though a dance may include a solo performance, it is the group movements that create the beauty of the dance.

Vivid and colorful costumes add to the visual effect of a dance. There are basically two types of costumes: *more* (moh-RAY), which is a grass skirt, and *pareu*, the colorful length of cotton. The more is the more elaborate costume. It is accompanied by a variety of creative natural accessories such as a belt sewn with shells, flowers, and seeds; a garland of flowers or shells; a flower headdress; and a bra for the women dancers. These accessories vary greatly every year. Women sling the grass skirt low on the hips to accentuate their hip movements, while male dancers tie theirs at the waist. For special events, the flower headdress is replaced by a tall elaborate headgear made of fibers, and male dancers add a short cape to the costume. Dancers also hold in their hands a tuft of fibers that resemble longish pompoms, called *ii*. The pareu, on the other hand, is worn with only a garland and flowers in the hair.

Four types of dances are performed in Tahiti today—*otea, aparima, hivinau,* and *paoa*. The best-known and oldest is the otea, and Tahitians look upon it as a symbol of their culture.

OTEA *Otea* (oh-TAY-ah) is performed for special events. For this reason, the dancers always wear the *more*. The larger the group of dancers, the more beautiful the dance is. Otea can bring together up to sixty dancers, and the minimum is six. The dancers form separate columns of men and women facing the spectators. They all move at the same time, and the formation remains

the same throughout the performance. Otea is physically very demanding and does not last more than six minutes. A performance usually consists of a series of otea lasting about fifteen minutes. When otea is danced by a group of men, it is a war dance, and the dancers often hold spears in their hands.

APARIMA The narrative dance, *aparima* (AH-pah-ree-mah), is sometimes accompanied by a song. Dressed in pareus, the dancers are placed in the same column formation as for otea. At least six men and women are required for this dance. Depicting scenes from daily life, such as fishing or preparing food, the dancers use their hands to mime their actions. The emphasis is placed on the hand movements, and the aparima is usually performed in a kneeling position or in a sitting position with legs tucked underneath.

HIVINAU Named from the English term "heave now" used by the nineteenth-century English-speaking sailors when lifting anchor, *hivinau* (hee-vee-NOW) is essentially a party dance. Children and old people can join in. When

Colorfully dressed men perform a traditional Polynesian dance at a resort on the island of Taha'a.

performed for an audience, hivinau brings together a mixed group of around twenty male and female dancers dressed in more. The dancers form two circles, men and women separately, with a singer and a group of musicians in the middle. The two circles are in constant motion, moving in opposite directions or both in a clockwise direction. The male singer sings a few lines, and the dancers answer with "*Ahiri a ha ahaha!*" This phrase does not have any meaning—it is only a shout of joy. A common subject for hivinau is fishing and the sea.

PAOA *Paoa* (pah-OH-ah) originates from tapa-making sessions, when a group of women sat down to beat tree bark into tapa cloth, singing and beating at the same time. Today the subject of the dance is usually fishing or hunting. The paoa dance group consists of a male singer, a large choral group of men and women, musicians, and one or two dancers. Depending on the occasion, the group wears more or everyday clothes.

PAINTING

Almost from the moment Tahiti was discovered by Europeans, the island was the subject of many paintings by visitors who wanted to record its landscapes and people. The first painter to depict scenes of Tahiti was Englishman William Hodges, who was part of Cook's second expedition in 1773. He made pictorial records of the ship's landing and scenes of daily life and drew portraits of Tahitian people, including Omai and King Pomare. The nineteenth century attracted more painters in search of inspiration. While Frenchmen Paul Gauguin and Jacques Boullaire were more interested in painting faces and expressions, Englishwoman C. F. Gordon Cumming painted beautiful watercolors depicting Papeete and other Tahitian landscapes.

Tahitian painting is no longer the domain of foreigners in search of exoticism. Several local painters have made a name for themselves through regular exhibitions, and the Association of Artists was created in 1984 to develop this art form. One of the best-known Tahitian painters was Rui Juventin (1916—1997), who actively promoted local painting. Because there is no tradition of painting in Tahitian society, artists tend to follow European

PAUL GAUGUIN

Wanting to escape the rat race of Western civilization is not a new urge. The French artist Paul Gauguin (1848–1903) was looking to do exactly that when he traveled to Tahiti in 1891. In France, he was in a desperate financial and personal situation. His marriage had failed and his career as an artist had stalled, despite him being at the epicenter of the Parisian art scene. He hoped the exotic culture of Tahiti would revive his creativity and rocket him to fame.

Arriving in Papeete, Gauguin was initially disappointed by how Westernized the French colony had already become. His desire for the "savage," or the primitive, closer-to-nature idyll, took him to the tiny town of Mataiea on the southern coast of Tahiti Nui.

There, he lived with a young vahine named Tehaamana, who was one of his favorite models. In this two-year period he produced eighty paintings, among them such masterpieces as Ia Orana Maria (Hail Mary), Woman With a Mango, Manao Tupapau (The Spirit of the Dead Keeps Watch), *and others. Life on Tahiti changed the artist's painting style as he embraced bolder, flatter colors, bright patterns, and "primitive" subject matter. Embued with a daydream-like sense of fantasy, his paintings from this time period evoke sensuality and freedom.*

Gauguin left Tahiti in 1893, hoping to sell his paintings in Paris. However, his exhibition of Tahitian paintings was a flop. Hoping to spark interest in his exotic paintings, he wrote a book titled Noa Noa, *about his blissfully erotic life in Tahiti. (Critics today believe some details were invented or at least exaggerated, as Gauguin was a known self-promoter.) He returned to Tahiti in 1895, but he was plagued by financial and health problems—thought to be syphilis—and his paintings took on a more pensive note. He died in the Marquesas in 1903, in abject poverty.*

Gauguin never achieved the popularity and financial success he dreamed of, but shortly after his death, his star finally began to rise in the international art world. Today he is recognized as one of the greatest artists of the nineteenth-century art. He had enormous influence on painters such as Henri Matisse and Pablo Picasso, and his work, particularly the Tahitian paintings, remains very popular today. In 2015, Gauguin's 1892 portrait of two Tahitian girls titled Nafea Faa Ipoipo (When Will You Marry?), *shown above, sold for close to $300 million, one of the highest prices paid for a single piece of art.*

models, and there are a variety of styles in their productions. These variations help enrich Tahitian art through painting.

LITERATURE

Just like painting, writing about Tahiti has traditionally come from European and American authors. The first piece of writing about Tahiti was Bougainville's myth-making account of his visit to the island. About a century later, Pierre Loti (whose real name was Louis-Marie Julien Viaud) wrote *Le Mariage de Loti,* a sad love story about a young French navy lieutenant and a teenage *vahine*. The book was an instant success (and is thought to have influenced Gauguin's decision to go to Tahiti.) Tahiti has also inspired much writing in English. After sailing to the Marquesa Islands and Tahiti, the American writer Herman Melville wrote of his adventures in the novel *Typee (1846)* and its sequel *Omoo* (1847), which were great commercial successes. In 1915, the young English poet Rupert Brooke spent three months in Tahiti, where he wrote one of the best of his early poems, "Tiare Tahiti."

Writers began creating literature in the Tahitian language only in the 1960s. It was written mainly by intellectuals in search of their cultural identity. Duro Raapoto (1948—2014) was a linguist, poet, and fervent defender of the Tahitian language. His poems deal with the difficulties of life and reveal the aspirations of the Polynesian people. John Mairai (b. 1945) uses theater to claim his Polynesian identity. His plays deal with the problems of daily life, and his caustic dialogues go down very well with his Tahitian audiences. Mairai was a friend of Henri Hiro, a prominent activist whose poetry sought to promote Polynesian culture in the 1970s and 1980s.

CARVING

Ancient Tahitians carved plain, realistic figures, either as statues or as ornaments. Tikis are wooden or stone statues that had a religious significance. Petroglyphs are scenes carved out of stone, depicting stylized characters or objects such as fish, turtles, or headdresses. Articles for daily use as well as those for ornamental purposes were sculpted into decorative designs. Combs, handles of fans, and bowls were intricately carved out of wood, basalt, bone, and shell.

Today's artists use the same materials. Precious woods such as sandalwood, rosewood, and *tou* (toh-OO) are carved into weapons, tikis, and flat dishes. Basalt stone is best for pestles and adzes.

There are a number of other crafts to be found in Tahiti. Tahiti is well known for its basketwork. Pandanus leaves are woven into hats, baskets, and mats. Tahitian artisans are experts at making flower garlands and headdresses. Shells and coral are made into beautifully intricate jewelry.

A tiki statue is carved in the traditional style.

INTERNET LINKS

http://www.sea.edu/spice_atlas/art_culture_atlas/musical_culture_in_french_polynesia
The music of French Polynesia is explored in depth in this report.

http://www.smithsonianmag.com/arts-culture/gauguins-bid-for-glory-226633/?page=5
The story of Paul Gauguin's life on Tahiti and his hopes for fame are told in this Smithsonian article.

http://www.thetahititraveler.com/general-information/art-culture/polynesian-dance-music
This travel site offers an overview of Polynesian dance and music.

LEISURE

An American surfer competes in the 2015 Billabong Pro Tahiti world surfing championship along the Teahupo'o coast.

11

S PORTS, DANCING, AND HAVING fun play an important part in the Tahitians' daily lives. They prefer leisure activities that involve a group of people because Tahitian society has traditionally been one of communal living. Getting together with a group of *fetii* (fay-tee-EE), even if only for a chat, is a source of great enjoyment. *Fetii* means "relatives," but the word is commonly used in a wider sense of close friends.

Teahupo'o (CHO-PO), a village on the southwestern coast of Tahiti Iti, is known in the surfing world for having some of the most thrilling waves in the world. They can reach up to 23 feet (7 m) and produce long tubes (inner cylinders) perfect for surfing. They are also among the most dangerous waves on earth. Teahupo'o translates loosely as "sever the head" or "place of skulls," and its "heavy" waves have claimed many a daredevil's life.

Locals and tourists alike enjoy relaxing at the beach.

THE LURE OF WATER

Outrigger canoe races are one way to celebrate Tahitian heritage during the Tiurai Festival.

Typical islanders, Tahitians love all activities related to water. Swimming is a favorite pastime, in rivers and the sea as well as under waterfalls. Picnics are very popular weekend outings because they combine family togetherness with the opportunity to go swimming. Favorite picnic places are the beach or an isolated *motu*.

Tahitians really come into their own when practicing water sports. Surfing is one of the oldest activities in Tahiti, having been documented by the first European visitors. Tahitian children do not need to go to the expense of buying fancy surfboards. They can ride the waves with anything at hand that is flat and light. The French national champions for surfing and windsurfing are usually Tahitians, and French surfers and windsurfers find that Tahiti is the ideal location in which to prepare for international competitions. Canoeing is another ancient sport. Tahitian outrigger canoes, called *va'a*, require several people to row, testing the team's strength, endurance, and sense of timing. Tahitians consistently rule as world champions in this sport.

SPORTS

The most popular sport is soccer. Well before the colonizers introduced the game to the island, the ancient Tahitians played a game called *tuiraa* (too-ee-RAH-ah), which consisted of kicking a ball into the opponent's camp. Competition was fierce among the districts, and the game was as popular as soccer is today. Soccer matches take place on weeknights and weekends at several soccer fields, the more popular ones being Fautaua Stadium and Stade Pater, both in Pirae, near Papeete. Enthusiastic crowds cheer on their favorite teams. Other team sports, such as volleyball and basketball, are also very popular, especially among the lower-income groups. Games of *pétanque* (pay-TAHNK), or French bowling, take place in rural areas.

More expensive sports, practiced mainly by the wealthy Demis and Popa'a, are tennis, golf, and horseback riding. Tennis courts are located mainly in the hotels and in Papeete as well as at private sports clubs. The Atimaono golf course was built on a former cotton plantation located between the lagoon and the mountains in a very colorful setting. There are two riding schools in

Local kids play beach soccer on the island of Moorea.

Cockfighting competitions draw big crowds despite being illegal.

Pirae that organize excursions into the mountains and the tropical forests.

Local spectator sports include Tahitian-style horse racing and cockfighting. Jockeys ride bareback, dressed in a brightly colored pareu and a flower headdress. Races are held on special occasions at the Pirae Hippodrome. Cockfighting, on the other hand, is illegal. However, fighting rings are out in the open, and the cockfights draw large crowds. Both horse racing and cockfighting take place on Sunday afternoons.

Sport fishing for marlin, shark, and other big game attracts many visitors to Tahiti.

GAMBLING

Tahitians of all social backgrounds like to gamble. In addition to lotto, there is another popular lottery that is organized by various groups year-round—the French national lottery, or *tombolas* (tum-BOH-lah). Winning numbers for the tombolas are drawn from a revolving drum, large sums of money are risked, and the draw is eagerly awaited by all concerned. Horse racing also gives rise to betting through the official pari-mutuel, which offers bets on horse and greyhound racing through the fixed-odds system. Even though payoffs are quite small compared with those of the tombolas, betting on horse races is still popular. Serious betting is also done on the outcome of cockfights, although this is, of course, illegal.

Casino-style gambling takes place in various hotels and under the cover of charity evenings organized by the Lions Club or other charitable organizations. Patrons play roulette and blackjack in a secretive atmosphere. Games of Asian origin, such as "big and small," or *van lak,* are also played, mostly illegally. Keno, a type of lotto, draws large crowds.

However, Tahitians do not need any betting structure to gamble. Many weekends are spent playing cards for cash wagers. The contests during Heiva i Tahiti (Festival of Tahiti) give rise to the most widespread betting of the year.

BRINGUE

Bringue (BRAING) means "having a good time," drinking, singing, dancing. There is no specific activity called bringue. Weddings, parties, discos, and other celebrations are all bringues. Some rural districts organize their own Saturday night bringue, usually as a fund-raising activity.

The music and dancing at a bringue are most often of Western inspiration. Pop songs and disco-style dancing are the norm. Sometimes the songs are in Tahitian, but the music is Western. Tahitian music is also played, and people dance, but the participants do not do the traditional tamure. Instead couples face each other, the woman swinging her hips and the man opening and closing his knees. Young and old have fun at the bringue. Children sing and dance with their parents and grandparents, and the bringue often does not end until late into the night.

INTERNET LINKS

http://www.thecoconet.tv/island-archives/traditional-sports-at-2016-heiva-i-tahiti
This site features a good video in English highlighting the traditional sports of the Heiva.

http://www.thetahititraveler.com/general-information/society/maohi-sports
Ma'ohi traditional sports are explained on this tourism site.

FESTIVALS

Modern dancers interpret native dances during the Heiva I Tahiti festival in Papeete.

12

THERE WAS A TIME WHEN TAHITI came close to losing its heritage of festive celebration. In the early nineteenth century, Christian missionaries and colonial authorities were shocked by the exuberant sensuality of traditional Tahitian dance and music, and quickly shut it down. Dancing was outlawed in 1819, but continued on clandestinely. Religious celebrations were marked with sobriety and modest everyday clothing replaced the scanty native costumes of grasses, shells, and flowers.

Those lost arts are now being revived under the heading of the islands' most remarkable festival, Heiva i Tahiti, sometimes called the Celebration of Life. The most popular activities during the Heiva are the competitions of traditional and modern sports, dancing, and *himene*, Tahitian choral singing.

Tahiti has the same public holidays as France, but festivals include those of the other segments of the population, such as Chinese New Year and Tiare Tahiti Day, which honors Tahiti's national flower.

HEIVA FESTIVAL

The most important and colorful festival of the year is Heiva i Tahiti, which means simply "Festival of Tahiti." Festivities start on June 29, the Anniversary of Internal Autonomy, and culminate on Bastille Day, July 14, cleverly linking two directly opposing inspirations: the nationalism of the Tahitian people and the colonial dominance of France. The festival comes from the French national day festivities during colonial times. While the governor and French administrators celebrated the occasion with a ball and a state banquet, the Tahitians were entertained with traditional games and cultural performances. In 1984, when Tahiti was granted full internal autonomy, the pro-French president of the Territorial Assembly hit upon the idea of bringing the start of the festivities forward by a few days to June 29 and combining the internal-autonomy celebrations with those of Bastille Day. However, the festival has expanded in many parts to take up the full month of July.

The highlights of the Heiva festivities are the competitions among contestants from the various districts and the outer islands. Traditional competitions are canoe racing, javelin throwing, stone lifting, coconut husking, basket weaving, tamure, and himene. Canoe races for both men and women are fiercely contested, with teams coming from all over the world. The canoes are carved out of a single tree trunk, and the race covers 4 miles (6.5 km) along the Papeete waterfront. One unusual event is the fruit-bearers' race. Male participants, dressed in pareus and flower headdresses, carry a colorful load of tropical fruits balanced on two ends of a banana tree trunk over a distance of 1.25 miles (2 km).

Less exotic competitions include bicycle, car, and horse races; pétanque games; and archery contests. Traditional tattooing sessions bring together young people who want to experience their cultural heritage. Bringues, or parties, are organized by regional organizations, and there is much dancing and feasting.

The Heiva celebrations also spotlight the works of native artisans. Palm-covered booths are crammed with the crafts of Polynesia. This is the largest gathering of craftspeople in French Polynesia. Hundreds of artisans gather to exhibit their artistry. Special events are held, including demonstrations of

January 1	New Year's Day
March 5	Missionaries Day
March April	Good Friday
March–April	Easter Monday
May 1	May Day
May 8	Victory Day
May	Ascension Day
May–June	Whit Monday (Pentecost Monday)
June 29	Internal Autonomy Day
Month of July	Heiva Festival
July 14	Bastille Day
August 15	Assumption Day
November 1	All Saints' Day
November 11	Armistice Day
December 25	Christmas

tifaifai quilting, weaving, and flower headdress making. The artisans dress in traditional attire, and there is always music and dancing.

July 2, which falls during the Heiva festival, evokes a totally different sentiment. This is the anniversary of the first French nuclear test at Moruroa in 1966, and commemorative ceremonies take place in Papeete.

BASTILLE DAY

Bastille Day on July 14 is France's national day. It commemorates the storming of the Bastille prison on July 14, 1789, at the height of the French Revolution. It symbolizes the end of the tyranny of the kings and a new era of freedom and democracy for the French people.

In Tahiti, the streets are decorated with French and Tahitian flags, and a military parade takes place in Papeete. Speeches are made, the republic is toasted, and fireworks light up the night sky. An all-night ball, today's version of the governor's ball, attracts revelers on July 13 in Papeete.

Nowadays the military parade is losing its importance. Since Tahiti gained internal autonomy, attention has focused more on the Heiva Festival, and parades of sports and cultural associations, which bring together *himene* groups, *tamure* troupes, and Chinese dancers, all dressed in their best finery.

RELIGIOUS FESTIVALS

The major Christian holidays are celebrated with fervor in Tahiti. Every Tahitian Christian attends church service, and the *himene* is even more beautiful on such occasions.

Christmas and Easter are the most important religious holidays. In Tahiti, of course, Christmas has a tropical flavor. Flowers are in full bloom, and they decorate houses and churches. Many church organizations hold a *bringue,* or music and dance party with food cooked in a traditional buried oven. Children polish their shoes so that *Père Noël* (pair noh-ELL), or Santa Claus, will leave presents in or on them.

Easter is ushered in by a late-night vigil. Some Catholics fast for forty days, the duration of Lent, a period when Christians get ready spiritually for the miracle of the Resurrection. Mass is said on the three days preceding Easter, with reenactments of Jesus Christ's last actions before being crucified. Chocolate eggs and Easter bunnies are given to children.

On All Saints' Day, families spend the day cleaning the graves of all the cemeteries at Papeete, Faa'a, Arue, and Puna'auia and decorating them with fresh flowers. Flower stands are set up all over the island, and people light candles in the cemeteries.

Assumption Day is celebrated only by the Catholic community. It marks the ascension of the Virgin Mary to heaven. The church service pays special attention to children, for they are all considered children of Mary.

A special holiday in Tahiti is March 5—Missionaries Day or Gospel Day. It commemorates the arrival of Protestant missionaries in 1797. Protestant churches hold a special service. All government offices and most businesses are closed on that day.

FAIRS

In addition to public holidays, there are a number of annual fairs and festivals celebrating various sports, arts, flowers, or regions. Taupiti O Papeete in May celebrates the town of Papeete. Miss Papeete is elected, and a carnival atmosphere reigns, with rides, games, and contests. The important activities take place on weekends.

The day honoring Tahiti's national flower, the *tiare Tahiti*, falls on December 2. Celebrators hand out flowers to people on the streets of Papeete, in the hotels, and at the airport. The highlight of this fair is an all-night ball with the flowers decorating the ballroom, the tables, and even the performers.

INTERNET LINKS

http://tahitinow.co.nz/about-tahiti/general-info/calendar-of-events
Many festivals are listed on this site, with links and contact information.

http://www.tahiti-tourisme.com/discover/events.asp
An up-to-date calendar of events for the Tahitian islands is found on this site.

http://www.tahiti-tourisme.com/discover/heiva-tahiti.asp
This tourism site explains the Heiva i Tahiti with photos and dance video.

FOOD

The vanilla orchid produces the pods that make Tahiti's distinctive vanilla.

13

W HEN EUROPEAN EXPLORERS discovered the Tahitian Islands, they thought they had found paradise on Earth—not only because of the region's beauty and near-perfect year-round climate, but also for its profusion of fish, fruits, and vegetables. Today, Tahitian cuisine reflects that native abundance. Coconuts, for example, are plentiful and their milk flavors sauces while the cream adds a lusciousness to desserts. Aside from other staples such as breadfruit, taro, and bananas, however, most of the fruits and vegetables used in daily meals have been introduced only in the past two centuries.

As a rule, Tahitian food is not spicy. Some dishes, especially such delicacies as raw fish and *popoi* (POH-poy), are an acquired taste. *Popoi*, a paste made from breadfruit, used to be the mainstay of the Tahitian diet but has now been replaced by the long loaf of French bread. Polynesians, Popa'a, and Chinese alike eat baguettes at every meal. The reasons are both practical and economic. Bread does not require any preparation, and it is one of the most filling and least expensive items

The vanilla orchid blooms for just one day, usually between July and August, during which time it must be pollinated—usually by hand—or it will not produce bean pods. Between 70 and 80 percent of Tahitian vanilla is grown on the small island of Taha'a, northwest of Tahiti in the Leeward Islands of the Society archipelago. For that reason, and for its pervasive vanilla scent, Taha'a is often called "Vanilla Island."

of food available. A typical Tahitian breakfast consists of bread, coffee, and perhaps some fruit.

The main meal of the day for the Popa'a population is lunch, consisting of meat, potatoes, and bread, sometimes accompanied by wine. Dinner is very light, usually leftovers from lunch. For the Polynesians and the Chinese, on the other hand, dinner is the heaviest meal of the day.

Restaurants are easy to find in Papeete, offering French, American, Italian, Chinese, and Vietnamese cuisine. They tend to be expensive—few Polynesians can afford to go out to a restaurant. Instead Polynesians head for the food wagons near the harbor. These small vans appear at around dinner time, serving cheap but good food—kabobs, French fries, and grilled meats.

Mobile food trucks begin selling their wares at dusk.

FISH

The favorite protein of Tahitians is fish, despite the fact that beef in Tahiti is quite cheap and of high quality. Perhaps this is because fishing is free and fish can be caught by anyone. About three hundred species of fish abound in Polynesian waters, but not all of them are edible. The armored soldier fish and the unicorn fish are prized by Tahitian gourmets. Sea bass and blue-spotted grouper release a wonderful aroma when grilled, while parrot fish, Napoleon fish, and jacks are best eaten raw.

Fish is eaten primarily in three ways: poached, grilled, and raw. Poaching is an easy way of cooking fish. Lagoon fish such as red mullet, grouper, sea bass, and jacks are cooked in a clear broth and drizzled with coconut milk before serving. For grilling, Tahitians traditionally use coral as fuel in addition to firewood. The fire is started with twigs and coconut husks, and small pieces of coral are placed on top. Once the coral pieces are hot and have turned brownish, the fish are placed directly on them for cooking. In addition to lagoon fish, mahimahi and tuna are grilled.

However, one of the most popular ways to consume fish is to eat it raw. The more conventional dish is a type of salad that contains tomatoes, carrots, and onions. The fish, preferably fresh tuna, is first soaked in salt water, then marinated in lime juice before being mixed with the salad vegetables and coconut milk. This dish is simply called *poisson cru* (pwa-son CROO), meaning "raw fish" in French.

Fafaru (fah-fah-ROO) requires a more intriguing preparation, and the Tahitian people are divided over its merits. Those who like it love it, while those who dislike it hate it intensely. Three or four fish are placed in an airtight coconut-shell container (or glass jar) and covered with seawater. The fish are left to soak in the water for two to three days. The liquid is sieved

Fresh tuna (*thon* in French) is sold by the roadside.

TAHITIAN VANILLA

Vanilla is said to be the world's favorite flavor. It's also the world's second-most expensive spice, mainly because it is so labor-intensive to grow, and because it grows in very few places in the world. One of those places is French Polynesia, particularly the Society Islands.

Native to Mexico, the vanilla orchid was introduced to the region by French colonizers in 1848. Growers developed it into a new variety called Tahitian vanilla and it became a major export. Because of its aroma profile, described as rich, fruity, and floral, Tahitian vanilla has been used primarily in perfume rather than in baked goods, though it can be used in place of any other vanilla.

Most of the world's vanilla is grown on Madagascar and on Réunion Island, (previously Bourbon Island), in the West Indies. These vanillas are often lumped together in one category called Bourbon vanilla. Mexican vanilla, which has a robust, smooth flavor, is even more expensive and is often considered the most prized.

Tahiti's vanilla production reached a height of 200 tons (181 metric tons) in 1939—much of it grown for export. However, it declined to a mere 4 tons (3.6 metric tons) in 1985, mainly due to the high costs of production. In 2010, newer, more efficient methods boosted production to almost 12 tons (10.9 metric tons).

Although Tahitian vanilla is a great point of pride and cultural identity in the islands, it no longer contributes much to the export market. Rather, it is an exotic specialty item aimed mostly at the tourist market.

through a fine cloth before being returned to the container, while the fish are thrown away. Fresh fish cut into cubes is then added to the liquid and left to marinate for at least six hours before the fafaru is ready for consumption. The marinating liquid lends a very pungent aroma to the dish, and it is definitely an acquired taste. Raw fish is eaten on Sundays, on special occasions, or when entertaining guests.

ALL-PURPOSE TREES

The fruit of the breadfruit tree

Called *uru* (OO-roo) in Tahitian, the breadfruit is probably the most useful tree in Tahiti. Ancient Polynesian legends tell of a man who turned himself into a breadfruit tree to save his family from famine. A single tree can produce fruit three times a year for fifty years, with as many as three hundred fruits each time. The starchy, easily digested fruit is rich in vitamin B and carbohydrates. In ancient times, to preserve the fruit for long voyages or to prevent famine, mashes were prepared; to make *mahi* (mah-HEE), fragments of pulp were cooked after they had been left to ferment in a trench covered with leaves and soil. The trunk of the breadfruit tree was hollowed into small outrigger canoes, the bark was beaten into tapa, and the latex was used as a glue for capturing birds. The latex is still used today as a plaster for healing fractures, sprains, and rheumatic joints.

The coconut palm is called the "tree of a hundred uses." Like the breadfruit tree, it provides shade and decorates the landscape. The edible parts are the nut and the heart of the young sprout. The nut provides coconut water and coconut milk. The husk can be plaited or twisted into a rope and provides an ocher dye for all kinds of decoration. The flesh (copra), when dried, is squeezed for oil, which is used to make scented skin oil, perfumes, and soaps. The palm fronds are woven into mats, hats, baskets, and roofs. The ribs are used for making skewers and brooms. The trunk of the coconut palm is sometimes used as building material, while the bark and the roots become ingredients of traditional remedies.

STAPLES

The traditional staple foods in the Tahitian diet are breadfruits, taros, *fei* (fay-EE) bananas, yams, and sweet potatoes. They are usually boiled or grilled and are eaten with fish and meats. *Fei* bananas are small, sweet, and red and must be cooked before being eaten.

Breadfruit is the most common staple. It is cooked whole over a wood fire, then peeled and eaten. A variation is to put the cooked breadfruit in a breadfruit leaf and hit it to form a paste. The breadfruit paste is then dipped into warm coconut milk before it is eaten. Breadfruit is also used to prepare *popoi*, another type of mash. The fruit is grated and wrapped in leaves before being boiled in water. Once cooked, the leaves are peeled off, lime juice and water are added, and the breadfruit is pounded for a while. *Popoi* is ready when the paste becomes elastic, and it is eaten with mashed bananas.

A market stall in Papeete showcases local fruits, including pineapples, bananas, and mangoes.

THE TAHITIAN OVEN

The Tahitian *ahimaa* (ah-hee-MAH-ah) is reserved for feasts called *tamaaraa* (tah-MAH-ah-RAH-ah), the equivalent of the Hawaiian luau, and can feed at least thirty people. More than a simple banquet, the preparation and eating of these feasts are an exercise in communal living. Men dig the pit while women wrap the food to be cooked.

The pit is 9 feet (2.7 m) long, 2 feet (61 cm) wide, and 1 foot (30.5 cm) deep. It is dug at around noon or even the day before in order for the food to be ready by dinnertime. Dry branches and twigs are used to cover the bottom. Basalt stones are then placed on top of the branches, and a fire is lit in the pit. When the stones are red-hot, green branches and a layer of green

Ciguatera is a type of food poisoning resulting from the consumption of toxic tropical fish. The fish themselves are poisoned by the Gambierdiscus toxicus *(G.T.) toxin, which is associated with algae growing on dead coral. The most frequently affected species are sea perch, emperors, groupers, parrot fish, Napoleon fish, and triggerfish—all of which form part of the Tahitians' staple diet. Deep-sea fish such as tuna, bonito, and mahimahi are never toxic. Every year around one thousand people become victims of ciguatera in French Polynesia.*

Ciguatera manifests itself in various symptoms, including a tingling sensation in the face and hands, vomiting, and diarrhea. The body feels weak, and the victim aches all over. Itching also occurs on the palms of the hands and the soles of feet, and for this reason, ciguatera is also known as "the itch." Severe cases can lead to death. No treatment exists for the toxin, and doctors can usually only treat symptoms, which can last for years.

banana leaves are spread over the stones, and the food is placed on top of the leaves. The whole pit is then covered with several layers of banana leaves, wet sacking, and sand. The *ahimaa* is left to bake for three hours.

The foods that go into the oven are wrapped separately in banana leaves so that they retain their individual flavors: suckling pig, fish, crayfish, crawfish, shrimp, *fafa* (fah-FAH)—chopped bits of chicken cooked with the tops of taro greens and coconut milk—a type of dessert called *po'e* (poh-AY), breadfruit, sweet potato, taro, and *fei* bananas. Everything is eaten off banana leaves with the fingers, accompanied by a coconut-milk sauce fermented with the juice of river shrimp. In addition to the *ahimaa, fafaru* and *popoi* are eaten at the *tamaaraa.* Drinks include beer, red wine, and water.

A *tamaaraa* is always accompanied by music. The band is usually made up of guitars, a ukelele, and a unique instrument made of a gasoline can tied to a broomstick with a piece of string. Participants wear flowers in their hair, and colorful flowers decorate the banquet table and surroundings. The *tamaaraa* is a perfect occasion for family and friends to gather in a convivial atmosphere.

TAHITIAN DRINKS

The ancient Tahitians used a rather interesting method to make an intoxicating drink. Fresh kava roots were chewed, usually by women, and the saliva-covered roots were then diluted in water to produce a type of liquor.

Beer is the most popular drink. The traditional Tahitian beer was made with fruit juices (orange or pineapple) to which water and sugar were added. It was bottled and left to ferment for four to five days, which caused the fizz in the drink. Today the local brewery produces a brand of European-style beer called Hinano from imported hops (a flower used to flavor beer), malt, and yeast. Only the water is Tahitian. Beer is considered a social drink because it is refreshing and inexpensive. It is always present during a gathering of *fetii*, and no *bringue* or *tamaaraa* is complete without it.

A man squeezes grated coconut meat in a cloth to release the coconut milk.

The most refreshing drink of all is undoubtedly fresh coconut water. It is the cheapest drink, after tap water. However, it is important to choose young fruits, which have sweet water. Once the nut has hardened, the water turns sour.

PAPEETE MARKET

Le marché (luh mar-SHAY), as Papeete's market is known, is housed in pretty new buildings located just one block from the waterfront. It is clean and free of unpleasant odors. Everything is available: bread, fish, meat, fruit, vegetables, coconut-oil soap, tikis, and pareus. The market reflects an earlier Papeete—earthy, vibrant, colorful, and full of amiable confusion.

The market is most crowded during the early morning hours on Sundays. The arrival of fresh fish at dawn marks the height of activity. Most of the market stallholders come from outside Papeete, and they arrive in trucks.

Many vegetable and fruit sellers come from the outer islands, and they stay in Papeete until all their stock is sold. Some stay with *fetii*, but most sleep in the large covered hall next to the market. In the evening, the hall is transformed into a huge municipal dormitory when the visitors spread out their mats for the night.

The colorful "Mapuru a Paraita," or Papeete Municipal Market, is a shopper's paradise for tourists and locals.

INTERNET LINKS

https://www.goway.com/travel-information/australia-south-pacific/tahiti/food-and-drink
This site provides a quick summary of Tahitian cuisine.

http://www.sea.edu/spice_atlas/moorea_atlas/the_vanilla_of_french_polynesia
An in-depth explanation of the history and production of Tahitian vanilla is provided on this site.

http://www.tahiti-tourisme.co.uk/about-tahiti/culture/cuisine
This short overview of Tahitian food includes a link to a recipe for poisson cru.

PO'E (TAHITIAN FRUIT PUDDING)

Po'e (POH-eh) is a popular fruit pudding. Originally the pudding was wrapped in banana leaves and baked in the fire pit. Coconut cream is the thick coconut milk that rises to the top of a can of coconut milk. Don't shake the can before you open it and you can skim it right off the top.

4 to 6 servings
6—8 ripe bananas, peeled and cut into chunks
½ cup (90 grams) brown sugar
1 cup (120 g) cornstarch
2 teaspoons vanilla
1-14 oz can (414 mL) full-fat coconut milk, unshaken and refrigerated for two or three hours.

Preheat oven to 375° Fahrenheit (190 Celsius). Puree the bananas in a blender or food processor. There should be enough puree to make 4 cups (480 g).

Mix together the brown sugar and cornstarch and add to the bananas. Add vanilla and process until smooth.

Butter a 2-quart (1.8 L) baking dish and pour in the puree. Bake for 30 to 45 minutes, or until the pudding is firm and bubbling. Remove from oven and allow it to cool. Cover with plastic wrap and refrigerate until well chilled.

To serve, cut the po'e into cubes and place into a large serving bowl or in individual bowls. Open the can of coconut milk and spoon the thickened cream from the top over the cubes of banana po'e. Sprinkle with a little more brown sugar.

PO'E VARIATIONS
Papaya, mango, pineapple, or other tropical fruits can be used in place of some of the bananas, as long as the fruit puree totals four cups. For juicier fruits, a little more cornstarch may be needed.

CHEVRETTES À LA VANILLE ET COCO (SHRIMP IN VANILLA COCONUT SAUCE)

4 servings
2 tablespoons olive oil
2 lbs (900 g) raw shrimp, peeled and deveined
1 vanilla pod, split lengthwise
½ cup (120 mL) rum
1 cup (240 mL) coconut milk
1 cup (240 mL) heavy cream
salt and pepper, to taste

Pat the shrimp dry. Heat the olive oil in a frying pan add the shrimp and stir-fry for 3 minutes or until they turn pink.

Remove them from the pan and set aside and wipe the pan clean.

Add the rum and the vanilla pod to the frying pan, bring to the boil and reduce to about 2 tablespoons.

Stir in the cream and coconut milk, and simmer until the mixture is reduced by half.

Scrape the seeds out of the vanilla pod into the cream mixture and discard the pod.

Season with salt and pepper.

Return the shrimp to the sauce and cook for 1 minute, stirring.

Serve immediately over cooked rice.

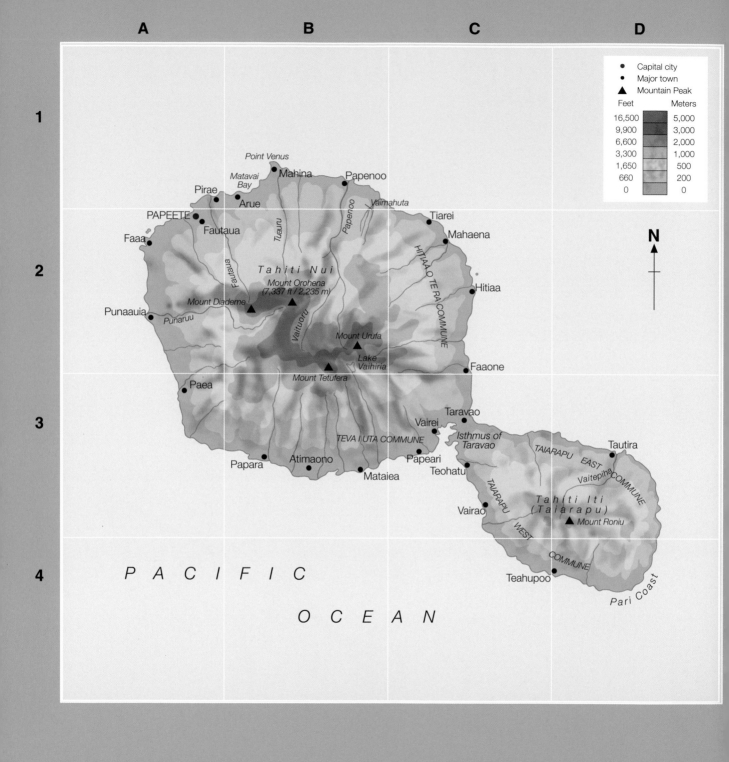

A   **B**   **C**   **D**

1

2

3

4

Capital city
Major town
▲ Mountain Peak

Feet	Meters
16,500	5,000
9,900	3,000
6,600	2,000
3,300	1,000
1,650	500
660	200
0	0

N

Point Venus
Matavai Bay
Mahina
Pirae
Papenoo
Vaimahuta
Arue
PAPEETE
Tiarei
Fautaua
Mahaena
Faaa
Tuauru
Papenoo
Hitiaa
Tahiti Nui
Vaituoru
Fautaua
Mount Orohena
(7,337 ft / 2,235 m)
Mount Diademe ▲
▲
Punaauia
Punaruu
Mount Urufa ▲
Lake Vaihiria
HITIAA O TE RA COMMUNE
Faaone
▲
Mount Tetufera
Paea
Taravao
Vairei
Tautira
Isthmus of Taravao
TEVA I UTA COMMUNE
TAIARAPU EAST
Papeari
Teohatu
Vaitepiha
COMMUNE
Papara
Atimaono
TAIARAPU
Mataiea
Tahiti Iti (Taiarapu)
Vairao
▲ *Mount Roniu*
WEST
COMMUNE
Teahupoo

P A C I F I C

O C E A N

Pari Coast

MAP OF TAHITI

ECONOMIC TAHITI

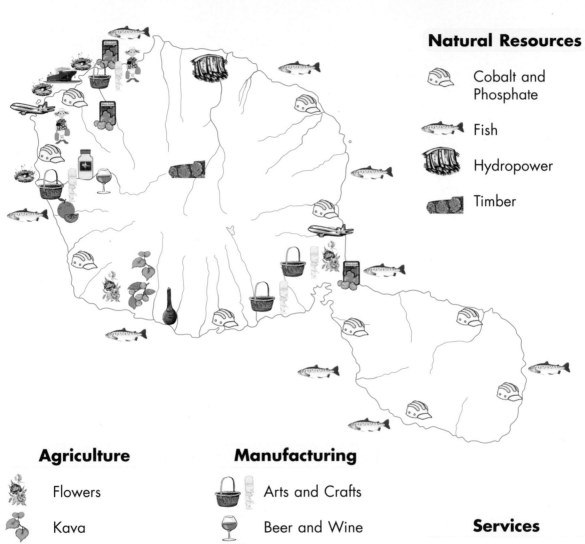

Natural Resources

- Cobalt and Phosphate
- Fish
- Hydropower
- Timber

Agriculture

- Flowers
- Kava
- *Noni*
- Oranges
- Vegetables

Manufacturing

- Arts and Crafts
- Beer and Wine
- *Noni* Juice
- Pearls
- Vanilla

Services

- Airport
- Sea Port
- Tourism

ABOUT THE ECONOMY

OVERVIEW

After growing at an average yearly rate of 4.2 percent from 1997—2007, the gross domestic product (GDP) stagnated in 2008 and fell by 4.2 percent in 2009, marking French Polynesia's entry into recession. GDP growth was positive in 2010—2012. In 2012, French Polynesia's tourism-dominated service sector accounted for 85 percent of total value added for the economy, employing 80 percent of the workforce.

Note: all statistics pertain to French Polynesia unless otherwise specified. All figures are estimates for the given year. Gross Domestic Product (GDP)
$7.15 billion (2012), official exchange rate

GDP GROWTH

2.4 percent (2012)

INFLATION RATE

1.1 percent (2013)

CURRENCY

French Pacific franc (XPF)
Notes: 500, 1,000, 5,000, and 10,000 XPF
Coins: 1, 2, 5, 10, 20, 50, and 100 XPF
1 USD = 112.82 XPF (January 2017)

INDUSTRIES

tourism, pearls, agricultural processing, handicrafts, phosphates

AGRICULTURAL PRODUCTS

Coconuts, vanilla, vegetables, fruits, coffee, poultry, beef, dairy products, fish

MAJOR EXPORTS

Cultured pearls, coconut products, mother-of-pearl, vanilla, shark meat

MAJOR IMPORTS

Fuels, foodstuffs, machinery and equipment

MAIN TRADE PARTNERS

France, South Korea, China, United States, New Zealand, Singapore, Australia

LABOR FORCE

114,300 (2012)

LABOR FORCE BY OCCUPATION

agriculture: 13 percent
industry: 19 percent
services: 68 percent (2013)

UNEMPLOYMENT RATE

21.8 percent (2012)

POPULATION LIVING BELOW POVERTY LINE

19.7 percent (2009)

CULTURAL TAHITI

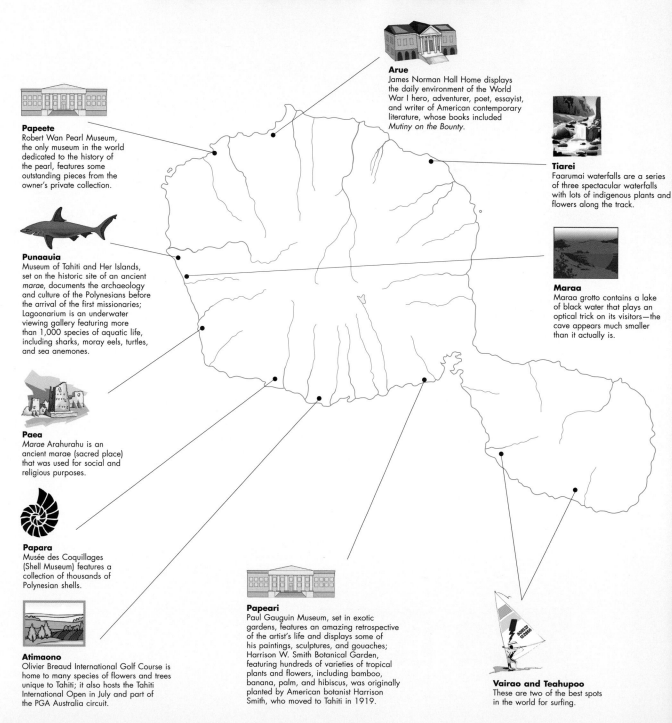

Arue
James Norman Hall Home displays the daily environment of the World War I hero, adventurer, poet, essayist, and writer of American contemporary literature, whose books included *Mutiny on the Bounty*.

Tiarei
Faarumai waterfalls are a series of three spectacular waterfalls with lots of indigenous plants and flowers along the track.

Papeete
Robert Wan Pearl Museum, the only museum in the world dedicated to the history of the pearl, features some outstanding pieces from the owner's private collection.

Maraa
Maraa grotto contains a lake of black water that plays an optical trick on its visitors—the cave appears much smaller than it actually is.

Punaauia
Museum of Tahiti and Her Islands, set on the historic site of an ancient *marae*, documents the archaeology and culture of the Polynesians before the arrival of the first missionaries; Lagoonarium is an underwater viewing gallery featuring more than 1,000 species of aquatic life, including sharks, moray eels, turtles, and sea anemones.

Paea
Marae Arahurahu is an ancient marae (sacred place) that was used for social and religious purposes.

Papara
Musée des Coquillages (Shell Museum) features a collection of thousands of Polynesian shells.

Atimaono
Olivier Breaud International Golf Course is home to many species of flowers and trees unique to Tahiti; it also hosts the Tahiti International Open in July and part of the PGA Australia circuit.

Papeari
Paul Gauguin Museum, set in exotic gardens, features an amazing retrospective of the artist's life and displays some of his paintings, sculptures, and gouaches; Harrison W. Smith Botanical Garden, featuring hundreds of varieties of tropical plants and flowers, including bamboo, banana, palm, and hibiscus, was originally planted by American botanist Harrison Smith, who moved to Tahiti in 1919.

Vairao and Teahupoo
These are two of the best spots in the world for surfing.

ABOUT THE CULTURE

Note: all statistics pertain to French Polynesia unless otherwise specified. All figures are estimates for the given year.

OFFICIAL NAME

Overseas Lands of French Polynesia

FLAGS

French Polynesia—two red horizontal bands encase a wide white band; centered on the white band is a disk featuring the French Polynesian coat of arms—a blue-and-white wave pattern depicting the sea, with a gold-and-white ray pattern depicting the sun; a Polynesian canoe rides on the wave pattern; the canoe has a crew of five represented by five stars that symbolize the five island groups; red and white are traditional Polynesian colors.

Tahiti—The flag of the island of Tahiti is the same as above, but without the disk in the center.

France—The flag of France is used for official occasions: three vertical bands of blue, white, and red.

TOTAL AREA

French Polynesia, 1,545,007 sq miles (4,001,550 sq km); Tahiti, 402 square miles (1,041 sq km) land

CAPITAL

Papeete, on the island of Tahiti

POPULATION

French Polynesia, 285,321 (2016); Tahiti, 183,645 (2012)

ETHNIC GROUPS

Polynesian, 78 percent; Chinese, 12 percent; local French, 6 percent; metropolitan (European) French, 4 percent

RELIGIOUS GROUPS

Protestant, 54 percent; Roman Catholic, 30 percent; other, 10 percent; none, 6 percent

MAIN LANGUAGES

French (official), 61.1 percent; Polynesian (official), 31.4 percent; Asian languages, 1.2 percent; other, 0.3 percent; unspecified, 6 percent (2002 census)

LITERACY RATE

Tahiti, 98 percent; smaller islands unavailable but probably lower

LIFE EXPECTANCY AT BIRTH

total population: 77.2 years
male: 74.9 years
female: 79.6 years (2016)

INFANT MORTALITY RATE

4.7 deaths/1,000 live births

TIMELINE

IN TAHITI	IN THE WORLD
600 CE First settlement of Tahiti.	
1767 Discovery of Tahiti by Samuel Wallis, who claims the island for the British crown.	**1530 CE** Beginning of transatlantic slave trade organized by the Portuguese in Africa
1768 Louis-Antoine de Bougainville visits Tahiti and claims the island for France, calling it New Cythera.	
1769 James Cook spends three months at Matavai observing the transit of Venus.	**1776** US Declaration of Independence
1788 William Bligh of the HMS *Bounty* arrives in Tahiti.	**1789–1799** The French Revolution
1790 Pomare I conquers all of Tahiti and becomes the first king.	
1812 Pomare II converts to Christianity.	
1834 French missionaries arrive.	
1842 French protectorate is proclaimed over Tahiti and Moorea.	
1844–46 The French–Tahitian War is fought.	
1847 Queen Pomare accepts French protectorate.	
	1861–1865 US Civil War
1866 Introduction of French legislation	**1869** The Suez Canal opens.
1880 The protectorate becomes a French colony.	
1885 Tahiti and the other islands in the archipelago become French Oceania.	

IN TAHITI	IN THE WORLD
1891 Paul Gauguin arrives in Tahiti and dies in 1903 on Hiva Oa.	
1914 Papeete is shelled by two German cruisers.	**1914–1918** World War I
1941–1945 Tahitian volunteers fight in World War II.	**1939–1945** World War II
1942 American military base established on Bora Bora.	
	1949 The North Atlantic Treaty Organization (NATO) is formed.
	1969 *Apollo 11* mission spaceflight; Neil Armstrong becomes first human on the moon.
1984 Tahiti is granted full internal autonomy.	**1991** Breakup of the Soviet Union
	1997 Hong Kong is returned to China.
	2001 Terrorists crash planes in New York, Washington, D.C., and Pennsylvania.
2003 Tahiti changes its status to French overseas community.	**2003** War in Iraq begins.
2004 Oscar Temaru becomes president; is ousted months later in a no-confidence vote; Tahiti becomes an overseas country of France.	
2005 Oscar Temaru is reelected president.	**2008** US elects first African American president, Barack Obama.
2014 Édouard Fritch becomes president of French Polynesia.	**2015–2016** ISIS launches terror attacks in Belgium and France.
	2017 Donald Trump becomes US president.

GLOSSARY

Afa Tahiti (AH-fah tah-hih-TIH)
Children of European and Polynesian parents

ahimaa (ah-hee-MAH-ah)
Food baked in an underground oven

breadfruit
A staple in the Tahitian diet; eaten boiled or grilled, the fruit has the taste and texture of bread

bringue (BRAING)
Party with singing, dancing, and drinking; literally, "having a good time"

Demis (deh-MEE)
Descendants of early marriages between Polynesians and Europeans

fafaru (fah-fah-ROO)
Raw fish marinated in seawater

fetii (fay-tee-EE)
Relatives, close friends

himene (hee-MAY-nay)
Singing; from the English word "hymn"

hupe (HOO-pay)
Mountain wind

Le truck (luh TRUCK)
Minibus used for public transport

maraamu (mah-rah-AH-moo)
Strong wind blowing from the southeast

marae (mah-RAH-ay)
Ancient place of worship

motu (moh-TOO)
Small island

Popa'a (poh-pah-AH)
A white person, usually a French person; literally, "foreigner"

popoi (POH-poy)
Breadfruit paste eaten with coconut milk

raau tahiti (rah-AH-oo tah-hih-TIH)
Traditional Tahitian natural remedies

Taata Maohi (tah-AH-tah mah-OH-hee)
Name by which Polynesian Tahitians refer to themselves; literally, "people of Polynesia"

tahua (tah-HOO-ah)
Traditional healer

tamaaraa (tah-MAH-ah-RAH-ah)
Large feast of *ahimaa*

tamure (tah-MOO-ray)
Tahitian dancing

tiki
A carved figure or image representing an ancient Polynesian god

Tinito (tee-NEE-toh)
Chinese

vahine (vah-HEE-nay)
Woman

FOR FURTHER INFORMATION

BOOKS

Bolyanatz, Alexander. *Pacific Romanticism: Tahiti and the European Imagination*. Westport, CT: Praeger Publishers, 2004.

Layton, Monique. *The New Arcadia: Tahiti's Cursed Myth*. Victoria, B.C.: Friesen Press, 2015.

Lonely Planet. *Tahiti and French Polynesia,* 10th edition. Franklin, Tenn: Lonely Planet. 2016.

Prince, Jan. *Tahiti and French Polynesia Guide*. New York: Open Road Publishing, 2005.

Salmond, Anne. *Aphrodite's Island: The European Discovery of Tahiti*. Berkeley: University of California Press, 2010.

Shackelford, George and Claire Freches-Thory. *Gauguin Tahiti*. Boston: MFA Publications, 2004.

Stanley, David. *Moon Tahiti*, 7th edition. Berkeley: Avalon Travel Publishing, 2011.

WEB SITES

CIA World Factbook. French Polynesia. https://www.cia.gov/library/publications/the-world-factbook/geos/fp.html

Encyclopaedia Britannica. Tahiti. https://www.britannica.com/place/Tahiti

Lonely Planet. French Polynesia. https://www.lonelyplanet.com/tahiti-and-french-polynesia

Radio New Zealand. French Polynesia news. http://www.radionz.co.nz/tags/French%20Polynesia

SEA Semester. Sustainability in Polynesian Island Cultures and Ecosystems. http://www.sea.edu/spice_atlas

South Pacific. Tahiti Travel Guide. http://www.southpacific.org/guide/tahiti.html

World Atlas. Tahiti. http://www.worldatlas.com/webimage/countrys/oceania/tahiti.htm

FILMS

Cousteau: Tahiti—Fire Waters. Atlanta, GA: Turner Home Entertainment, 1998.

Mutiny on the Bounty. Warner Brothers, 1962.

____. Warner Brothers, 1935.

Tahiti: French Polynesia. Huntsville, TX: Educational Video Network, Inc., 2006.

MUSIC

Heart of Tahiti. Gnp Crescendo, 1999.

Magic of the South Seas. Arc Music, 2000.

Tahiti Dances to Drums of Bora Bora and Papeete.Hana Ola Records, 2004.

BIBLIOGRAPHY

BBC News. French Polynesia territory profile. http://www.bbc.com/news/world-asia-16492623
____ French Polynesia profile—Leaders. http://www.bbc.com/news/world-asia-16494639

Bowermaster, Jon. "The Fragile Island that Tahiti Used to Be." *The New York Times*. February 18, 2007. http://www.nytimes.com/2007/02/18/travel/18explorer.html

Captain Cook Birthplace Museum. "Omai the noble savage." http://www.captcook-ne.co.uk/ccne/themes/omai.htm

Conese, Jackie. "The Vanilla of French Polynesia." Sea Education Association. http://www.sea.edu/spice_atlas/moorea_atlas/the_vanilla_of_french_polynesia

Layton, Monique. *The New Arcadia: Tahiti's Cursed Myth*. Victoria, B.C.: Friesen Press, 2015.

Lonely Planet. French Polynesia. https://www.lonelyplanet.com/tahiti-and-french-polynesia

Radio New Zealand. "Paris to up Tahiti nuclear debt payment." September 2, 2016. http://www.radionz.co.nz/international/pacific-news/312402/paris-to-up-tahiti-nuclear-debt-payment

Smith, Erickson. "Subsistence Subsiding: Eighty Years of Change in French Polynesia's Fisheries," Atlas for Sustainability in Polynesian Island Cultures and Ecosystems, Sea Education Association, Woods Hole, Mass. 2013. http://www.sea.edu/spice_atlas/fakarava_atlas/subsistence_subsiding_eighty_years_of_change_in_french_polynesias_fisheries

St. Fleur, Nicholas. "How Ancient Humans Reached Remote South Pacific Islands." *The New York Times*, November 1, 2016. https://www.nytimes.com/2016/11/02/science/south-pacific-islands-migration.html?_r=0

Tahana, Jamie. "The battle continues, 50 years after first test at Mururoa." Radio New Zealand, July 4, 2016. http://www.radionz.co.nz/international/pacific-news/307804/the-battle-continues,-50-years-after-first-test-at-mururoa

United Nations Committee of 24. The United Nations and Decolonization. http://www.un.org/en/decolonization/specialcommittee.shtml

Vargas Llosa, Mario. "The men-women of the Pacific." *Tate Etc.* issue 20: Autumn 2010, September 1, 2010. http://www.tate.org.uk/context-comment/articles/men-women-pacifi

INDEX

INDEX